Mothercraft and Infant Health

Mothercraft and Infant Health

A Sociodemographic and Sociocultural Approach

Doris Peyser Slesinger
University of Wisconsin

LexingtonBooks
D.C. Heath and Company
Lexington, Massachusetts
Toronto

Library of Congress Cataloging in Publication Data

Slesinger, Doris P.
  Mothercraft and infant health.

  Includes bibliographical references and index.
   1. Infants—Care and hygiene—Wisconsin—Longitudinal studies.   2.
Mother and child—Wisconsin—Longitudinal studies.   3. Infants—Care and
hygiene—Social aspects—Wisconsin—Longitudinal studies.   4. Family—
Wisconsin—Longitudinal studies.   I. Title. [DNLM: 1. Infant care—
Methods.   2. Mother-child relations. WS 113 S632m]
RJ102.5.W6S55   649'.4   81–47181
ISBN 0–669–04562–4   AACR2

Published simultaneously in Canada

Printed in the United States of America

International Standard Book Number: 0–669–04562–4

Library of Congress Catalog Card Number: 81–47181

This book is dedicated to persons in three generations who have helped me understand what mothercraft is all about:

My parents	*Harold Louis Peyser*
	Helene Fantel Peyser
The father of my sons	*Jonathan Avery Slesinger*
My sons	*Jeffrey Slesinger*
	David Slesinger
	Paul Avery Slesinger
and my husband	*Edward Wellin*

Contents

List of Figures   xi

List of Tables   xiii

Foreword   *David Mechanic*   xvii

Preface and Acknowledgments   xix

Chapter 1   **Introduction**   1

Mothercraft   4
Sociodemographic Components   5
Sociocultural Factors   6

Chapter 2   **Methodology**   9

General Design   9
Choosing the Sample   10
Choosing the Families   11
Training the Interviewers   11
Confidentiality   13
Time Schedule   13
Final Sample after 17 Months   14

Chapter 3   **Description of the Sample**   17

Geographic Location of Sample   17
Demographic Characteristics of the Sample   20

Chapter 4   **Measuring Mothercraft**   27

Introduction to Components of Mothercraft   27
Mothercraft Appraisal Score (MAS)   29
Components of Health Knowledge   32
Attitudes toward the Medical System   34
Interrelationships among the Mothercraft
   Measures   37
Mothercraft Measures and Sociodemographic
   Characteristics   39

Chapter 5   **Measuring the Infant's Health and Development**   41

Preventive Health Measures for Infant   41
Height and Weight Records   43
Record of Baby Illnesses   46
Record of Baby Accidents   46
Nurse's Health Assessment   47
The Denver Developmental Screening Test
    (DDST)   48
Diet of Infant   49
Summary of Infant Health Measures   58
Sociodemographic Characteristics and Infant
    Health   58
Relationship between Mothercraft and Infant
    Health Measures   59

Vignettes of Selected Families   63

Chapter 6   **Sociodemographic Characteristics of Mothers
and the Relationship to Mothercraft and Infant
Health**   103

Sociodemographic Characteristics and
    Mothercraft Appraisal Score   104
Sociodemographic Characteristics and Medical
    Attitudes and Health Knowledge   105
Sociodemographic Characteristics and Infant
    Health   106
Relationship between Mothercraft and Infant
    Health, Controlling for Effects of
    Sociodemographic Characteristics 110
Mothercraft Component Score (MCS)   111

Chapter 7   **Sociocultural Setting and Its Relationship to
Mothercraft and Infant Health**   117

Measures of Social Integration   118
Social Integration and Mothercraft Appraisal
    Score   119
Sociodemographic Characteristics and Social
    Integration   122
Relationship between Integration and
    Mothercraft, Controlling for
    Sociodemographic Effects   124

Relationship between Mothercraft and Infant
Health Measures, Controlling for the
Effects of Significant Integration Variables   126
Comparison of Effects of Sociodemographic
versus Social-Integration Variables on the
Relationship between Mothercraft and Infant
Health   127

Chapter 8   Summary and Discussion   135

Model   136
Method and Sample   137
Findings   138
Implications   141
Future Research   144

**Appendix A   Wave 1 Interview Schedule and Mothercraft
Appraisal   147**

Appendix B   Surrogate Cases   169

**Appendix C   An Evaluation of Component Items in
Mothercraft Appraisal Score   175**

**Appendix D   An Experimental-Control Test of Effects of
Participation in Study   179**

References   189

Index   197

About the Author   202

List of Figures

1-1   Model of Mothering as Related to Infant Health   5

2-1   Time Schedule of Project   14

3-1   Location of Study Families in Milwaukee
        Neighborhoods   18

3-2   Location of Study Families in Wisconsin   20

4-1   Picture Shown to Mothers to Identify Potential
        Dangers for a Child   35

5-1   Distribution of Weight for Age, by NCHS Standard
        Percentiles   44

5-2   Distribution of Length for Age, by NCHS Standard
        Percentiles   44

5-3   Distribution of Weight for Length, by NCHS
        Standard Percentiles   45

List of Tables

2–1	Nurses' Reasons for Choosing Family to Be in Study	12
2–2	Residential Mobility of Sample Mothers over 17-Month Period	15
2–3	Age of Infants at Each Interview	16
3–1	Population Characteristics of Eight Milwaukee Neighborhoods in which Study Families Resided, 1975	19
3–2	Population Characteristics and Summary of Health Facilities in Four Wisconsin Counties in which Study Families Resided	21
3–3	Selected Demographic Characteristics of Infants and Mothers, by Urban-Rural Residence	22
4–1	Appraisal Scores at Three Time Periods, Based on Sixty Common Items at Three Waves	33
4–2	Health-Knowledge Score at Time 1 and Repeated at Time 3	34
4–3	Pearsonian Correlation Coefficients between Components of Mothercraft	38
4–4	Pearsonian Correlation Coefficients between Sociodemographic Characteristics and Mothercraft Measures	39
5–1	Record of Well-Baby Checkups, by Residence of Mother	42
5–2	Immunization Records of Infants, by Residence of Mother	43
5–3	Distribution of Total Number of Infant Illnesses, Reported by Mothers Over 20-Month Period	47
5–4	Accidents to Infant, Reported by Mother	47
5–5	Distribution of Infants by DDST Scoring at 3, 12, and 19 Months	49
5–6	Type of Milk Infant Receiving at 3 Months	50

5-7   Diet of Infants at 3 Months   51

5-8   Diet of 3-Month-Old Infants, by Percentile of Weight
           for Length   53

5-9   Frequency of Feeding for Infants on "Regular"
           Schedules at 3 Months   53

5-10   Food Intake of 20-Month-Old Infants Classified by
           the Four Food Groups   54

5-11   Proportion of 20-Month-Old Infants Having
           Recommended Intake of Four Food Groups   55

5-12   Proportion of 20-Month-Old Infants Having
           Recommended Intake of Specific Combinations of
           Food Groups   56

5-13   Proportion of 20-Month-Old Infants Having
           Recommended Intake of Each Food Group   56

5-14   Frequency of Mention of Fats, Oils, and Sugars for
           20-Month-Old Infants   57

5-15   Frequency of Eating   57

5-16   Pearsonian Correlation Coefficients between
           Sociodemographic Factors and Six Infant Health
           Measures   59

5-17   Pearsonian Correlation Coefficients between
           Mothercraft and Infant Health Measures   60

6-1   Multiple Classification Analysis between
           Sociodemographic Characteristics and Mothercraft
           Appraisal Score   104

6-2   Pearsonian Correlation Coefficients between
           Sociodemographic Characteristics and Measures of
           Medical Attitudes and Health Knowledge   106

6-3   Multiple Classification Analysis between
           Sociodemographic Characteristics and Infant Health
           Measures   108

6-4   Multiple Classification Analysis between Mothercraft
           Measures and Infant Health Measures, Controlling
           for Sociodemographic Factors   112

6–5   Multiple Classification Analysis between Mothercraft
        Component Score and Measures of Infant Health   114

6–6   Multiple Classification Analysis between
        Sociodemographic Characteristics and Mothercraft
        Component Score   115

7–1   Multiple Classification Analysis between Social
        Integration Measures, Mothercraft Appraisal Score,
        and Mothercraft Component Score   121

7–2   Pearsonian Correlation Coefficients between
        Sociodemographic Characteristics and Measures of
        Social Integration   123

7–3   Multiple Classification Analysis between Social
        Integration Measures and Mothercraft Scores,
        Controlling for Sociodemographic Factors   125

7–4   Multiple Classification Analysis between Infant
        Health Measures and Mothercraft, Controlling on
        Social-Integration Variables   128

7–5   Comparison of the Effect of Sociodemographic and
        Social-Integration Factors on Infant Health Measures
        in Additive Models (Multiple Classification Analysis)   132

D–1   Medical Conditions during First Twenty Months
        of Life   181

D–2   Infant's Health Status as Rated by Nurse   183

D–3   Birthweight as Growth-Chart Percentiles   184

D–4   Length for Age   184

D–5   Weight for Age   185

D–6   Weight for Length   185

The National Research Council's Advisory Committee on Child Development, after a four-year study, concluded that there was a need for new types of research in child development:

> Although the emphasis in developing and improving social indicators is on standardization and replication, there is a real need for the development of new methods of measurement to capture aspects of child development that cannot be assessed adequately with existing instruments. The most pressing need is certainly in psychological and social development. Behavior observation techniques that are practical and reasonably economical to apply in large-sample, limited-time surveys are also needed.

> Child-development researchers should devote more attention to the design and analysis of studies that measure changes over time in the condition of children and the causes of those changes. This means sacrificing some of the precision of the laboratory in order to learn about children's behavior and development in natural environments.
> (National Research Council 1976, pp. 109–110)

Foreword

It is widely recognized that the quality of mothering in early life sets the stage for the child's future development and later-life chances. Mothering is, of course, a broad concept and ranges from maternal interest, attention to the physical needs and sensory stimulation of the child, to teaching moral values, skills, aspirations and achievement motives, and much more. While the concept is difficult to pin down, there is universal agreement that the behaviors to which it refers have great importance for the health and welfare of the child.

In this book, Doris Slesinger examines the relationship between quality of mothering in 123 mother-infant pairs and its relation to the health and health care of the infant in the first 20 months of life. Researchers concerned with the child's development have devoted considerable attention to mothering, but Dr. Slesinger's focus on how mothering is embedded in the sociodemographic and sociocultural condition of the family is a relatively unique focus. She demonstrates clearly that mothering is not simply a personal quality for good or bad but is closely connected to poverty, education, and other social and environmental circumstances. Such evidence makes clear that the future health of children depends not only on interventions designed to improve capacities of the individual mother, but on interventions aimed more broadly toward ameliorating social conditions that result in neglect and apathy, and over time in poor health and diminished vitality.

Dr. Slesinger's study is an important exploratory venture aimed at developing appropriate methods for investigating the complex interrelationships among the sociocultural environment, mothering, the health-care system, and the health and development of the child. She recognizes the necessity for prospective investigation and the limitations of even 20 months of followup for detecting developmental deficits even in the case of impoverished families. Most of our current knowledge derives from either cross-sectional or more-intense short-term observation or from large aggregate statistical investigations based on official records as in the study of infant mortality. Instead, Dr. Slesinger has focused on observing mother-child units over time and linking the observations made to later health outcomes.

As her study indicates, the patterns of behavior to be described are varied, the available methodologies uncertain, and the links between environment, behavior, and health status enormously complex. There is an important need for refining our techniques of investigation and our conceptual approaches. The book explores alternative approaches, identifies new variables of importance, and portrays the strategic problems we will have to deal with in the future if we are to continue to improve our understanding of family interaction and health.

This book is of interest as much to the practitioner as to the researcher. It identifies social, familial, and behavioral parameters of importance to public-health nurses and other healthworkers who serve mothers and their young children and alerts health professionals to criteria by which they can sharpen their observations of critical factors and direct their efforts more effectively. Thus, practitioners, as well as researchers, should be grateful for Dr. Slesinger's efforts to explore new territory and to make further work more directed and less difficult for those who follow in her path.

David Mechanic
Professor of Social Work and Sociology
Graduate School of Social Work
Rutgers University

Preface and Acknowledgments

My concern with the health and development of infants awakened after the birth of my first son. At the time, I was an ignorant parent, totally dependent on my pediatrician to tell me what was right, what was wrong, what mattered, and what was insignificant in the long run. After giving birth to two additional sons, I realized that one learns from experience—but also discovered that every baby is unique. Each baby had his own reactions to me; and I, in turn, reacted to each baby differently.

Between giving birth and raising children, I pursued advanced degrees in sociology. Graduate study trained me to generalize from specific situations, conceptualize my thoughts, and apply methodological techniques to research topics I encountered.

Thus developed my interest in studying infant births and deaths and causes of pre- and postnatal mortality. I first investigated this area as a demographer and used linked infant birth and death records as a data source. The variables available to correlate with infant deaths were limited to specific demographic facts and medical conditions so that associations could be made, but explanations were speculative. For example, there was a high correlation between low birthweight and infant death, and low birthweight and nonwhite infants. But the question remained, why were nonwhite infants more likely to be born with low birthweight? These statistical data could not answer this question. My frustration with this type of analysis for this research problem led me to design this study in order to obtain more in-depth information on the handling of infants in the home and in the sociocultural environment. In addition, I realized the importance of a longitudinal rather than cross-sectional design to address this problem.

I developed the conceptual framework and ideas for this study while I was a postdoctoral fellow funded by the Robert Wood Johnson Foundation at the Center for Medical Sociology, University of Wisconsin-Madison, under the direction of David Mechanic.

Funding for fieldwork and analysis was provided by the Research Committee of the Graduate School, University of Wisconsin-Madison, and the Institute for Research on Poverty. Throughout the study the Department of Rural Sociology has been supportive of my work in numerous ways, for which I am grateful, and I would like to acknowledge the support of the College of Agricultural and Life Sciences as well as of the University of Wisconsin-Extension. Additional support in the final stages of writing was provided by a Ford Foundation grant, "An Interdisciplinary Approach to the Study of Motherhood,'' awarded to the Women's Studies Research Center at the University of Wisconsin-Madison.

Three graduate students in sociology assisted in the preparation of data for analysis, and the analysis itself: Alexandra (Sandy) Wright, Patricia Guhleman, and Maxine Thompson. Special thanks go to Sandy for her careful work on the components of the Mothercraft Appraisal Index. Pat's work on the vignettes of the mothers was thoughtful and valuable. Luise Cunliffe of the Institute for Research on Poverty also deserves special appreciation for programming indexes and merging data files from three separate interviews.

I also appreciate the suggestions of health professionals with whom I consulted at different stages: Mary Beckman, RN, consultant with the Maternal and Child Health Section of the Wisconsin Department of Health and Social Services, who advised on appropriate rural sites for the study; Rosemary Vahldick, RN, public health nursing consultant with the Wisconsin Department of Health and Social Services, who reviewed a pretest copy of the interview schedule; and Charles Schoenwetter, M.D., University of Wisconsin Medical School, who generously contributed to the interpretation of the health and growth records of the study infants.

Four colleagues were most helpful in reading drafts of the manuscript: David Mechanic, Karl Taeuber, Maxine McDivitt, and Edward Wellin. Their suggestions were carefully addressed, often gratefully accepted, and occasionally rejected. The faults remaining in the final copy are solely mine. Special appreciation goes to my beloved husband, Edward Wellin. His support, insights, and intellectual thoroughness kept me honest and enthusiastic throughout the study.

I now turn to the public-health nurses who were intimately involved as interviewers in this endeavor, without whose interest and dedication this study would not have left the drawing board. I am indebted to them for their careful observations and recordings, their willingness to learn new interviewing methods using a standardized instrument, and their dogged persistence in tracking down very mobile families. I also appreciate the cooperation of the responsible administrative units: in counties, the County Board of Health; in the city of Milwaukee, the commissioner of the Milwaukee Health Department, Constantine Panagis, M.D.; in

Clark County: Public Health Nursing Service. Lois O. Guest, supervising nurse, and Anne Filitz

Marathon County: Health Department. Adrienne Weisbrod, director of Public Health Nursing; Agnes Leitheiser; Eunice Luepke; Laura Nest; and Lois Ramaker

City of Milwaukee: Health Department. Bureau of Public Health

Nursing. Carol M. Graham, superintendent; Cecile Loreck, assistant superintendent; Margaret Arzt; Ruth Brennan; Cheryl Brown; Regina Cotter; Lolita Hinz; Rosie Joecks; Mary Leiske; Marie Mueller; Margaret Olszewski; and Jill Wood Paradowski

Waushara County: Public Health Nursing Service. Marie Millington, supervising nurse; Ann Buck; Rebecca Gillings; Vivadell Olsen; and Dwight O. Schafer

Wood County: Public Health Nursing Service. Janet Menshing, director; Beatrice Albert; Kathryn Bowden; Joyce Carpenter; Joan Hanson; Irene Johnson; Maxine Joling; Eileen Longmore; Terri Mayer; Lucy Weiler; and Janice Winters.

I want to express my deep respect and appreciation for my research specialist, Eleanor Cautley, who has been involved in the project since it went into the field. Together we learned about differences in fielding a study in urban and rural areas, following specific families over time, analyzing data at three time points, and ironing out computer and data problems. Eleanor supervised the coding of materials, all typing, and performed most of the computer work. She handled technical and administrative problems with ease; no problem was insurmountable. And what is perhaps most important, we discussed interpretations of specific mother-child pairs, and together developed better ways of presenting the results. I am fortunate to be associated with such a creative and thoughtful assistant.

The careful typing of innumerable drafts as well as final copy was due to the talents of Linda Clark and Chris Fox. A number of women coded the interviews for computer processing, most notably Linda Tuchman and Ruth Landis. Ruth also prepared the first draft of the matched-sample design that appears in appendix D.

I want to close with special thanks to the mothers who were involved in the study. Too often sociologists and other researchers obtain all the information needed for their research from willing respondents and then disappear from the scene. I am afraid that I have also been guilty of this. Although I have held feedback sessions with the nurses and am pleased that participation in this study has sharpened their awareness and perceptual skills for community health work, none of the mothers knows how valuable a part they played in this study. Fortunately, the public-health nurses provided services, aid, and advice while following the families for the two-year period. So, in some respects, the families gained a little from being involved in the study. However, I hope that the readers of this book, through their community involvement, will help me repay the debt, if not to the original respondents, to other mothers who are struggling to raise healthy children in poverty environments.

1

Introduction

This study evolved from the author's interest in combining two areas of research, each conventionally dealt with by distinct subdisciplines. One stems from the author's longstanding interest in infant mortality, from a demographic perspective; the other is an interest in the postneonatal period, when everyday patterns of handling and caring for an infant presumably have significant effects on health and development. The latter interest reflects a medical-sociological perspective.

With respect to infant mortality, research in the 1960s pointed to the existence of pockets of high infant death rates in the United States such as among the American Indian population, rural blacks in the South, and teenage mothers in cities. Despite ethnic, residential, and other differences, these pockets have in common the presence of poor and medically under-served women. It was thought that because of these pockets, the U.S. infant death rate was not able to drop to the levels reported from Sweden, Netherlands, or Japan (Shapiro, Schlesinger, and Nesbitt 1968). It was also thought that if these women could have the advantages of their counterparts in the American mainstream, their infant death rates would fall, resulting in this nation's rate falling to the low levels of the Scandinavian countries. Overall infant death rates have fallen since that time, but the areas with high mortality rates still remain (National Center for Health Statistics 1977a).

An analysis of linked birth and death certificates in Wisconsin (Slesinger 1973a; Slesinger and Travis 1975) revealed that whereas the major correlates of infant death could be identified (that is, low birthweight, extreme ages of the mother, history of incomplete pregnancies), we knew little about the causal factors behind low birthweight or histories of fetal loss. Some nutritionists suggested poor prenatal diet; others suggested poor diets of the women during puberty. Some physicians as well as health researchers (Kessner et al. 1973) felt that poor prenatal care added to the risk. Some suggested low birthweight in blacks was genetic because the U.S. statistics showed that, in general, black babies weighed one-half pound less than white babies at birth (MacMahon 1974). A recent comprehensive review of causal factors relating to pregnancy outcome, however, lists a half dozen more factors besides those mentioned above. (National Research Council

1

1970). It is clear, however, that infant deaths are more likely to occur in poverty environments. The poor are more likely than the middle class to have poor nutrition as well as substandard living conditions and inadequate medical care.

Infant deaths are often divided into two groups: neonatal (birth through the first month) and postneonatal (the second month of life through the first year). In developed, industrialized countries, it is generally agreed that neonatal deaths are more likely to be caused by congenital and birth problems, whereas the deaths occurring in the postneonatal period are more likely to reflect sociocultural and environmental conditions. If this is accurate, then statistics for blacks and whites should indicate more postneonatal deaths among black infants than white infants, given the higher incidence of poverty and poor environmental conditions among the former.

The statistics bear this out. In 1975 the overall U.S. infant death rate was 16.1 deaths per thousand live births. For whites it was 14.2, and blacks 26.2, 1.8 times the white rate. Of all deaths, about 28 percent were in the postneonatal period. The black postneonatal rate, however, was over twice the white rate (National Center for Health Statistics 1978, table 25). Thus the chances were greater in the black population for an infant to die, and to die in the postneonatal period.

In the United States, however, the numbers of infant deaths are relatively small (16 per thousand births, on the average), and the number of deaths in the postneonatal period even smaller (4.5 deaths per thousand births). Therefore, I turned my attention to related but more common events that occurred in the first year of life—infant morbidity. But how could one relate social and economic factors to morbidity? Data are lacking on child illnesses unless they are among the reportable communicable diseases or are serious enough to be seen by a doctor; data on child accidents, other than those seen at doctors' offices or hospitals, are similarly lacking.

I designed an exploratory study that would address infant morbidity and relate it to possible causal factors in the home. The home included the physical setting but clearly had to focus on the child's caretaker—the provider of the emotional and cognitive environment that is assumed to be crucial to normal development of an infant. Assuming that postneonatal mortality is the extreme condition of postneonatal morbidity, I believe that by examining differentials among physical, social, and emotional environments, it might be possible to uncover aspects of infant care that could be related to postneonatal infant death.

In fact, we know very little about the daily home life and treatment of children; as the National Research Council has noted (1976, pp. 14–15):

> The data necessary to construct a reasonably complete picture of American families—how they raise their children and how they cope with the daily problems presented by a complex urban society—are virtually nonexistent. Such data as do exist must be pieced together from many sources, and in-

evitably they provide an incomplete picture. The lives of children are even harder to describe, except when circumstances bring children into contact with institutions outside the family.

Certainly, much work has been done on nurturing and child development, and an enormous volume of both biological and social-science investigations have attempted to link maternal care and child development.

However, most work has looked at the effects on children of extreme maternal deprivation, intense social isolation, and severe maternal personality disorders. The well-known work of Harlow and associates with monkeys (Harlow, Harlow, and Hansen 1963; Harlow, 1965; Jensen and Tolman 1962; Seay, Hansen, and Harlow 1962; Seay and Harlow 1965) and others with human infants (Spitz 1945; Goldfarb 1945, 1947; and Provence and Lipton 1962) have clearly shown that poor development and lack of "thriving" occur when infants are deprived of maternal care. Thomas, Chess, and Birch (1968) have shown that mothers' personality disorders also affect the child's development.

Other researchers investigate more "normal" populations but select samples of children from clinics or case records (Haggerty, Roghmann, and Pless 1975; Kempe and Helfer 1972; Giovannini and Billingsley 1970), or do not share with the reader the exact source of case sampling (Tulkin and Cohler 1973; Tulkin and Kagan 1972).

If we are to consider seriously the prevalence of poor child nurturance and child neglect, we must turn our attention to what happens in families in "normal" populations. That is, we need to examine how children fare in families with unsatisfactory nurturing and not limit ourselves to cases of extreme deprivation. Neither should we focus only on children and families on patient or client list of various types.

An exploratory study was designed to investigate exactly this: the effects of poor-quality mothering on infants in some typical or normal population. The research is termed "exploratory" because measures of quality of mothering had to be developed; cases of inadequate mothering had to be identified; and ways of following the family over a period of time had to be devised.

In our society, nurturing is found in the family unit, and the biological mother is the person usually responsible for the home environment and source of infant care. Although much has been said in recent years about the role of the father, the increasing numbers of communal families with shared childrearing responsibilites, and even homosexual marriages, it is undeniable that early child nurturing rests in good part on what is done and not done by the infant's biological mother. When the biological mother does not satisfactorily perform the mothering role, it is essential for the child's well-being to have a "surrogate" mother replace the biological mother.

This book reports the results of first steps to delineating the problem, developing valid and reliable instruments, and evaluating the procedures for hypothesis testing at a later date. In Glaser and Strauss's (1967) term, we follow the principle of "grounded theory." That is, a basic model is proposed, then data gathered that will refine and expand the model, depending on the results of the exploratory research. The proposed model is depicted in figure 1-1.

Starting with the dependent variable in figure 1-1, we see that an infant's health will be affected by the quality of mothering (mothercraft) the infant receives. In turn, the quality of mothering will be affected by various sociodemographic and sociocultural characteristics.

Previous research has led the author to believe that a mother's ability to nurture an infant is affected to a good extent by two elements: The first is the structural constraints that evolve from economic and demographic factors, and the second is the social environment that provides social supports.

Mothercraft

The concept of mothercraft, or mothering, resists precise definition. It is used here to include the following components: how the mother manages the child's physical environment; the mother's physical care of the child (rest, dress, cleanliness, health care); her emotional and cognitive handling and stimulation of the child; mother's personal characteristics that affect interaction with the child, for example, mother's feelings of dependency, apathy, futility, and verbal-communication ability; and mother's level of basic health knowledge, including awareness of safety hazards in the child's environment.

Based on extensive work in the area of child neglect, Polansky has developed instruments for evaluating maternal characteristics on the basis of home visits. His work has produced a "childhood level-of-living" scale and a "maternal-characteristics" scale for measuring the "current maturity of a woman's functioning" (Polansky, De Saix, and Sharlin 1972). These identify such personality dimensions as apathy-futility and childlike impulsivity and dependency, two specific characteristics that Polansky relates to poor mothering. The verbal-communication aspect was also found to be an important component in identifying poor mothering (Polansky, De Saix, and Sharlin 1972; Tulkin and Kagan 1972). Polansky's scale to measure maternal characteristics has been tested on both a rural population (Polansky, Borgman, and De Saix 1972) and an urban one (Hepner and Maiden 1971), and has been found to discriminate between competent and less competent mothers. An adaptation of Polansky's work is the basis for a Mothercraft Appraisal Score in this research.

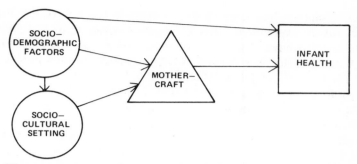

Figure 1-1. Model of Mothering as Related to Infant Health

Sociodemographic Components

Among the demographic factors that affect quality of mothering are the age of the mother at the time of the birth, her previous childbearing experiences, how much money she has to live on, and how much formal education she has had.

We noted previously the relationship between a mother's very young or very old age and the risk of infant mortality. Current concern with teenage childbearing is now producing research on the effects of mother's immaturity on the health of the child (Menken 1972; Baldwin 1976).

Large family size has been negatively related to physical health of the infant (Grant 1964), and the suggestion has been made that the child in the crowded home may be deprived of necessary infant-mother contact (Lieberman 1970). Seeking medical care for children has also been negatively related to family size. McKinlay (1972) notes that various British studies suggest that women with four or more children underutilize child-welfare, prenatal, and postnatal facilities. Morris, Hatch, and Chipman (1966) noted in a sample of low-income women that the more children a mother had, the fewer immunizations the study infant received.

The wantedness of a birth by the mother has also been related to health of the child (David 1971; Pohlman 1965, 1969). Unwantedness has been linked to mental disorder in the child (Menninger 1943; Lieberman, 1964) and psychiatric patients from large families have been found more often to be high-birth-order children (Barry and Barry 1967; Farina, Barry, and Garnezy 1963; Schooler 1964), suggesting the possibility that such children were either unwanted or received less attention than low-birth-order children or both. Beck (1970) has postulated a link between unwantedness and child abuse based on data of Silver, Dublin, and Laurie (1969) and other students of abuse. A study of adult outcomes of Swedish births in which the mother had been denied a request for abortion found that members of the experimental group were more likely to have received psychiatric care, to have achieved lower educational outcomes, and to have been more often the recipients of public assistance between the ages of 16 and 21 (Forssman and Thuwe 1966).

Various surveys have indicated that a child's receipt of medical care varies directly with family income. In addition, children in poverty-level families are less likely to receive well-baby checkups and immunizations (Bullough 1972; Morris, Hatch, and Chipman 1966, National Center for Health Statistics 1965, 1977c). Garbarino's work has attempted to demonstrate on an aggregate basis a strong link between economic deprivation and child maltreatment (1976, 1978).

Sociocultural Factors

The second element is sociocultural. Here we are interested in the cultural environment that the infant enters; the social supports and networks mothers have within and outside their households; what contacts they have with various societal institutions such as schools, employers, medical institutions, and the church. This component is measured by the composition of the household, use of community resources, and interaction patterns with friends and relatives.

Support was found in previous research on urban black mothers (Slesinger 1973b) for the hypothesis that the more the mother was integrated into a social unit, be it a primary family or church or PTA activities, the more likely she was to obtain preventive health care for herself and her children. This was true when the effects of socioeconomic status were removed. Mother's social isolation has been associated with child abuse (Gil 1970), as well as stress among unwed mothers (McClannahan 1967).

Of specific interest here is the association of social isolation with health utilization. Bullough (1972), Slesinger (1973b), and Mellinger, Manheimer, and Kleman (1967) independently note the direct relationship between social integration and the mother's propensity to seek medical care. Morris, Hatch, and Chipman (1966) note that mothers who feel socially isolated and powerless are likely to get less preventive care for their children than mothers of the same socioeconomic level who are not alienated.

Another aspect of social environment that has been addressed is the quality of family stability in the home. While no clear relationship with socioeconomic status is in evidence, the social maturity and general physical health of the infant appears to be related to family stability (Werner et al. 1967; Spence et al. 1954). Haggerty and Alpert (1963) note that more streptococcal infections appeared in children from families that had recently undergone stressful events than in children from families with no stressful events. Haggerty and colleagues also note in a prospective study in which mothers kept health diaries that family stress appeared to increase utilization of medical services, especially among children (Haggerty, Roghmann, and Pless 1975, pp. 142–146).

In summary, this study addresses the subject of infant health from a sociological perspective. It first asks, "What are the effects of sociodemographic and sociocultural conditions on the quality of mothering?" and then asks, "What are the effects of the quality of mothering on infant health?" Previous work has indicated substantial support for the significance of mother-infant interaction on the health of the infant. What is unique about this study is the attempt to measure the impact of social factors on the infant's health through the mediating variable of mothercraft.

In order to achieve its objectives, the present research requires:

1. *A prospective study design.* The study needs to assemble longitudinal data on each child, starting with the postneonatal period and ending after sufficient time to investigate the effects of poor home conditions, including poor mothering, on the child's health and development.

2. *A way to objectively evaluate the handling and care of the child.* This will necessarily involve qualitative ratings that can reflect the perceptions of trained observers but in a form sufficiently standardized to permit ratings to be compared from one observer to another, and one home to another. The development of this rating schedule is not only useful for research purposes but also would be valuable for public health nurses and community workers to utilize for early detection of poor mothering skills.

3. *A sample of "normal" families* at or below the poverty level, which would include a range of mothercraft patterns, some of which would be rated as poor mothering. Most studies of child-care evaluations have been conducted with children with special needs (Thomas, Chess, and Birch 1968) or of convenient samples, for example, upper-middle-class families near a university (Thomas et al. 1963). The present study is based not on problem families, nor homes with exceptional problems such as severely emotionally disturbed mothers, nor on known cases of child abuse, nor on infants with severe health problems. It is based on a group of women, many living at or below poverty level, who have recently given birth.

This book is arranged in the following order. Chapter 2 discusses the methods used to choose the sample and study families; procedures used in choosing and training the interviewers, and a description of the original sample and its attrition over the 17-month period. Chapter 3 notes the geographic location of the mothers, and the demographic characteristics of both the mothers and infants are described. Chapter 4 elucidates six components of mothercraft. Specific items to measure each are listed and the relationship between sociodemographic characteristics of the mothers and their mothercraft scores is noted. Chapter 5 describes various measures of infant health and development that are used in the study. The relationship between the socidemographic characteristics of mothers and measures of infant health are discussed as well as the relationship between mothercraft and infant health measures.

In the Vignettes, eleven families from the study are selected and described in detail, providing information on the mother, infant, and family members throughout the 17-month period. Most of the cases were chosen to illustrate the effects of structural sociodemographic conditions such as poverty, young age, low educational attainment, or poor social-support systems, on mothering scores and the various measures of infant health. Most of the cases describe poor mothering, although two cases are included that illustrate poverty conditions but good mothercraft.

Chapter 6 examines the relationship of mother's education, poverty status, race, age, and rural-urban residence with respect to mothercraft scores, medical attitudes, health knowledge, and infant health. Chapter 7 examines two types of social integration, primary and secondary. Then their relationship to mothercraft scores and infant health are determined. Chapter 8 reviews the purpose, model, and methodology of the study; discusses major findings; and specifies implications for policy and future research.

2 Methodology

General Design

As noted in chapter 1, the purpose of the study is to measure mothering ability among a group of women who have recently given birth and to evaluate the effects of mothercraft on the health of the infant over time. Major problems existed in sampling because the outcome variable—child health and development—would be known only after some time had passed and because inadequate mothering is a difficult concept to both measure and locate in a random selection of recent mothers. Because of the exploratory nature of this research, a decision was made to design a sample that was based on case screening, yet which basically would represent mothers in urban and rural settings who face a variety of social and structural conditions suggested in the literature to affect quality of mothering (Polansky, Hally, and Polansky 1975).

Once the infants and mothers were chosen, the design called for following these families until the babies were approximately 18 months old. The data to be obtained concerned both the health and medical-utilization patterns of the infant and the mother; a physical and developmental assessment of the infant; and a set of socioeconomic and cultural facts about the mother and her family. Therefore, the likely interviewers were public health nurses, who needed to be trained in interviewing techniques, rather than social-survey interviewers, who would not be able to weigh, measure, and examine infants, and conduct the developmental screening test. Three home visits by the nurses were planned, when the infants were approximately 3, 12, and 18 months old. Each visit included a structured interview by the nurse, physical examination of the baby including weight and height measurement, and the administration of the Denver Developmental Screening Test. A copy of the first interview schedule is presented in appendix A.

After the nurses left the household, they were asked to fill in a mothercraft-appraisal form based on their observations and personal interaction experience. This became one of the main measures of the quality of mothering.

The methodology for this type of study—a combination of home interviews and observations—has been used previously (Spence et al. in Newcastle on Tyne, 1954; Polansky, Borgman, and De Saix in Appalachia,

1972; Brown and Rutter in London, England, 1966) with reasonable success. There is considerable criticism leveled against using *only* self-reporting
through interviews and questionnaires (Yarrow 1963), especially in the body
of literature on child-rearing behavior. This research avoids this problem by
supplementing self-reporting in interview material with observation of
actual behavior at the time of the home visits.

Choosing the Sample

Because measures of infants' health will include utilization of medical
facilities, two types of geographic areas were included: a metropolitan area,
where medical personnel and facilities for child care were ample, and a nonmetropolitan area, where both accessibility to and existence of medical
facilities for pediatric care were minimal.

Four rural counties and the city of Milwaukee were chosen as sites for
this research. The Bureau of Public Health Nursing of the City of Milwaukee Health Department has had a policy for a number of decades for
public health nurses to routinely visit the homes of *all* babies born to
residents of the city of Milwaukee within two weeks to two months after the
birth. At that time the public health nurse gives the mother a copy of the
birth certificate. If permitted, she conducts a neonatal assessment and in-
vites the mother to discuss any problems she may be having. She also is used
as a health-information resource for the rest of the family such as a problem
with another child, the husband, or some other family member. This neonatal visit gives the nurse the opportunity to evaluate the household, to see
if there are any serious problems, and to offer assistance from the health
clinics in the city or other agencies that might assist the family. This was an
excellent way of screening families for this research project.

The Bureau of Public Health Nursing divides the city of Milwaukee
into 90 geographic areas. Three of these districts were basically comprised
of low-income families. Because the likelihood was greater of finding poor-
quality mothering in poverty areas, the choice of babies was restricted to
these areas.

The four rural counties were chosen from among Wisconsin rural counties on the basis of the reputation of the county's public health department's
interest in maternal and child health. The head of the Wisconsin Department of Public Health Nursing was consulted to locate areas where the
nurse supervisor in the county was interested in maternal and child health.
Preliminary discussions were held with some county nurse supervisors, and
four counties were chosen.

A procedure similar to that used in Milwaukee was attempted in order
to choose babies from poverty families in rural areas. This was not as
simple. The rural county health departments have, by and large, no pro-

gram of home visiting mothers of newborns. In fact, in some counties the nurses were not familiar with women in the community who had had a recent birth. Therefore, different methods were used. Some nurses looked at the birth certificates that were filed at the county courthouse. Others investigated a teen-pregnancy program in a high school. Others talked to social-service workers in order to get names of mothers who had had a recent birth and were on welfare. Another obtained referrals from a high-risk prenatal clinic.

The results of this process led to the voluntary involvement of 10 Milwaukee public health nurses and 20 rural public health nurses. Each city nurse was asked to locate 10 babies from her district, and each rural nurse was asked to locate 3 in her area.

Choosing the Families

Public health nurses were asked to locate families with a newborn where mothering was likely to be poor. As mentioned previously, this was to be determined after an initial screening visit. In Milwaukee nurses were able to evaluate the home environment when they made a routine neonatal visit. In the rural areas there was no such program. Therefore, the nurses asked for suggestions for characteristics that might produce families appropriate for the study. Based on previous research, some suggestions given were: very young mothers, the presence of a number of small children closely spaced, unstable marital situation, and very poor families. In addition, the babies were to be approximately 3 months old at the time of the interview, and the mothers had to be willing to participate in the study.

At the time of the first interview, each nurse was asked to write a paragraph on why she chose a particular family. The reasons the nurses gave fell into five categories. They were: personality and behavioral characteristics of the mother (41 percent); known problems with baby or another child (23 percent); family problems (11 percent); isolation from the larger community (9 percent); and a group of miscellaneous reasons, none of which included evidence of poor mothering (16 percent). Table 2-1 breaks these groupings into finer distinctions.

The final sample consisted of 148 babies born between 7 April 1974 and 26 February 1975. Of these, 101 babies were located in Milwaukee, and 47 in the four rural counties.

Training the Interviewers

For each group of nurses, an orientation-and-training meeting was held before any interviewing took place. At the first meeting emphasis was given

Mothercraft and Infant Health

Table 2-1
Nurses' Reasons for Choosing Family to Be in Study

	Percent (N = 123)
Characteristic of Mother	41.4
Young, inexperienced, immature	14.9
Emotional problems	8.8
Lack of self-confidence	6.8
Dependent	4.1
Slow to accept advice, obtain medical care	3.4
Low intelligence	2.0
Passive, apathetic	1.4
Problems with Baby or Older Children	23.0
Problems with older children	11.5
Emotional neglect of child	8.8
Continuous health problems with baby	2.7
Family problems	10.8
Large family	5.4
Very poor	3.4
Marital problems	2.0
Isolated from Community	8.9
New resident of community	3.4
Isolated	2.0
Mixed racial parentage of baby	1.4
Strong subcultural group attachment	1.4
Language barrier	.7
No "Mothering" Reason	16.3
Needed another case	6.1
Example of "good" low-income mother	3.4
Receptive to nurse	2.7
Other	4.1
Total	100.4

to choosing the sample families, interviewing techniques, observation techniques, and recording information. Nurses are used to *giving* information, not just listening and absorbing information. This required a certain reorientation in their training because in this project they had to ask questions, be given information, and not react in any evaluative way. They had to learn to accept uncritically what a person said, even if the comment was "wrong" or they disapproved of it. At each training meeting, we went over the interview carefully question by question including the purpose of each question and each section in the interview. After they had completed two interviews, we reconvened and went over the problems they had been having, clarified some of the questions, and discussed in detail what kinds of impressions and other information we wanted that was not included in the interview schedule itself. This was included in the "thumbnail sketch" section at the end of the interview where the nurse was able to write her impressions, information not included in the interview, and comment on anything that she felt was relevant. This process was repeated after each wave of interviews.

A tool for the nurse's training for this study was developed prior to the beginning of interviewing. There was considerable pretesting of the interview schedule and appraisal instrument. Interviews were conducted by nurses with poverty mothers whose babies were a little older than the 3 months required for the study. At this time two interviews were videotaped, after obtaining the mother's written consent. After editing, the tape ran 40 minutes and was included in the training-and-orientation meetings with the nurses to illustrate certain techniques and problems likely to be encountered in the interviews.

Confidentiality

Because of the longitudinal nature of the study design, the names of the mothers and babies had to be recorded for future contacts. To maintain confidentiality, the following arrangements were made with each department of nursing at the beginning of the study: A set of blank but numbered interview schedules were sent to each department of nursing. The supervisor assigned a number to the study family. From that point, the number was the only way the family was identified in the research project. Each department of nursing kept the key to the numbers in its confidential files. Thus the nurses had access to the department's files, but the researchers only knew the cases by number.

Time Schedule

The time span of this project lasted over three years. Figure 2–1 depicts the time periods of the various stages of work.

The study infants were born between April 1974 and February 1975. Pretesting of the various components of the study were carried out in June through August of 1974. Interviewer training began in October of 1974, and the interviewing followed for approximately five months. Most of the first-wave interviewing was completed by the end of March 1975. The second-wave training started in June of 1975 in Milwaukee, and interviewing proceeded through November; in the rural areas, training commenced in August, and interviewing lasted through January of 1976. The third-wave interviewing started in February of 1976 and proceeded through July of 1976. Most of the babies had reached the age of 18 months or older by June

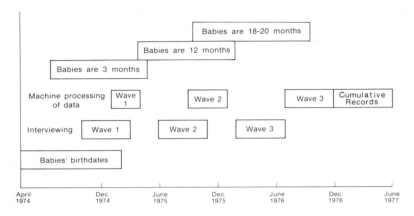

Figure 2-1. Time Schedule of Project

of 1976. The coding of each set of data was performed after the interviewing in each wave was completed. Final coding on the third wave was completed by December of 1976. The machine processing began at that time, and the final three waves of interviews were assembled and compiled by spring of 1977.

Final Sample after 17 Months

Sample deterioration occurred over the year-and-a-half period for two reasons: (1) residential mobility of families and (2) removal of infant from home.

Residential Mobility

The residential movement of the study families was considerable. Of the 148 families, only about 40 percent remained at the same address throughout the study. When the mother moved within the city or to another part of Wisconsin, all but one was followed and interviewed at the new location. When, however, she moved out of the state, she was dropped from the sample. Table 2-2 shows the mobility status of the families.

The "other" group consists of three mothers who refused to be interviewed at the second or third wave, and one mother whose infant died shortly after the first interview.

Table 2-2
Residential Mobility of Sample Mothers over 17-Month Period

Mobility		Number	Percent
Did not move		61	41.2
Moved within state		67	45.3
Once	40		
Twice	17		
Three or more times	10		
Moved out of state		11	7.4
Moved, unable to locate		5	3.4
Other		4	2.7
Total		148	100.0

Removal of Infant from Home

Some of the study families were under surveillance by the Division of Protective Services because of the poor relationships of the parents and children. In three cases, the baby was moved to a foster home. In an additional two cases, the baby moved to the grandmother's home and no longer lived with the mother.

In all cases we tried to keep the child in the study. In some cases the nurse was able to interview the foster mother and the natural mother separately. This was not always possible mainly because the foster parent was not a permanent placement, but a temporary one, and the nurses were not permitted to follow the infant into the foster home.

As mentioned previously, the difficulty in locating cases for this study varied from rural to urban location. Thus there was a range of ages of babies at each interview, although the study design called for interviews when the baby was 3, 12, and 18 months old. Table 2-3 displays the range of ages of infants at each interview and the mean age of the rural and urban samples. The rural infants, on the average, were slightly older at each interview than the urban infants. However, because medical information about each child was cumulated over the entire period for most of the outcome measures, the actual age of the infant at each interview is less important than the fact that data were gathered at three time periods and were reported for a 17-month time period.

On the average, the families were in the study for approximately 16.4 months, and the babies were approximately 20 months old at the time of the final interview.

Table 2–3
Age of Infants at Each Interview

First Interview		Second Interview		Third Interview	
Age (Months)	Number	Age (Months)	Number	Age (Months)	Number
1	2	11	10	17	6
2	27	12	40	18	19
3	58	13	45	19	39
4	23	14	15	20	30
5	10	15	9	21	16
6	2	16	2	22	9
10	1	18	1	23	3
	123	22	1	26	1
			123		123
Mean age	3.20		12.94		19.63
Rural	3.72		13.26		19.21
Urban	2.96		12.80		19.82

To summarize the evolution of the final sample, 148 mother-child pairs were selected and interviewed. At the end of the 17-month period, 123 mother-child pairs remained in the sample. Five additional cases were completed with "surrogate" mothers. These women were foster mothers or maternal grandmothers who were then responsible for the care of the infant.

Of the 20 families who were lost to the study, 11 moved out of the state, 1 infant died, 5 moved and were not located, and 3 refused to continue to participate. The child who died was 4 months old, and the cause of death was listed on the death certificate as Sudden Infant Death Syndrome.

The remainder of the analysis will be conducted with the 123 families who remained in the study for the 17-month period. It should be noted that some of the most serious cases of inadequate mothering were lost to the study because their problems were so great. The Division of Protective Services (Milwaukee) removed children from 5 homes and placed them under a surrogate mother's care. These cases are discussed in appendix B.

3

Description of the Sample

Geographic Location of Sample

Wisconsin was chosen as the site for this research. It is a state with over 4,500,000 residents, but it has only one city and surrounding area with over 1 million people. Life in the urban and rural areas is different, as in all states. The cities have higher densities of population, more industrial activity, and a wealth of medical services, both public and private. Rural areas are more likely to be more sparsely populated, with public services as well as medical services often lacking or available at greater distances. Because of the differences in environment and life-styles, this research includes an urban sample and a rural sample.

Urban Sample

The urban component was located in the industrial city of Milwaukee, a city of about 700,000 population. Many poor families live in a compacted area close to the center of the city. The families chosen by the nurses were located in 28 census tracts or eight community neighborhoods (Beverstock and Stuckert 1972) (see figure 3–1). Statistics from these neighborhoods, by and large, indicate that the population was likely to be poor, black, crowded in density and relatively young. Table 3–1 shows some characteristics of these neighborhoods and the number of study families chosen from each.

The Milwaukee area has ample medical facilities. There were 1.8 physicians per 1000 population in 1973, with 64 pediatricians practicing in the county. All study families were within 10 miles of a general hospital. Very rarely did it take more than 15 minutes to go to a doctor or clinic.

Rural Sample

The rural component was chosen from four different counties: Wood, Marathon, Clark, and Waushara (see figure 3–2). Table 3–2 contrasts some

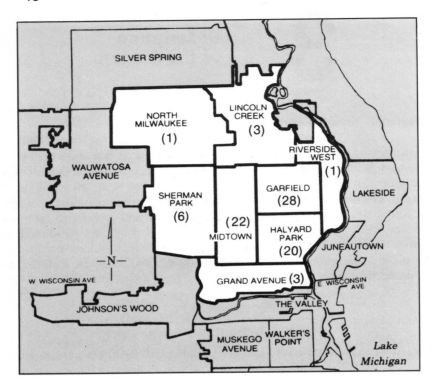

Figure 3–1. Location of Study Families in Milwaukee Neighborhoods

demographic and medical characteristics of these counties. All are considered by the U.S. Bureau of the Census as nonmetropolitan counties. That is, they have no city of 50,000 or more population or are not adjoining and economically tied to a county with such a large city. On the other hand, the four rural counties represent different types of rural areas: Wood and Marathon Counties have larger populations, with a number of cities over 2500 included. The other two, Clark and Waushara, are almost totally rural, have more aged in the population, and lower birth rates. Their medical facilities are meagre and are located at a sizable distance from the residents. There are no pediatricians practicing in Clark and Waushara Counties. Wood County, on the other hand, contains a large established and well-known group-medical practice, the Marshfield Clinic, which is a resource for the residents of the area as well as for those living a considerable distance away. Only in Wood County do most of the study families live within a 10-mile radius of a hospital.

Table 3–1
Population Characteristics of Eight Milwaukee Neighborhoods in which Study Families Resided, 1975

Characteristics	Milwaukee Total	Garfield Avenue	Grand Avenue	Halyard Park	Lincoln Creek	Midtown	North Milwaukee	Riverside West	Sherman Park
Total population	669,014	34,935	30,385	20,321	34,624	41,960	42,135	16,656	46,286
Population per square mile	10,299	17,462	13,211	10,421	9,538	16,717	8,512	9,102	12,857
Percent black	18.5	91.3	13.8	89.6	69.6	67.7	9.3	20.9	6.7
Age distribution (percent)									
Under 20	33.8	49.5	22.7	43.8	41.4	49.3	27.8	30.4	29.9
20–64	54.9	44.8	62.1	47.4	51.3	44.6	55.9	56.7	53.6
65 or older	11.3	5.7	15.2	8.8	7.6	6.1	16.3	12.9	16.5
Median age	29.5	20.6	30.5	22.4	24.9	20.6	37.1	27.7	30.9
Percent of 1969 median income	100.0	80.6	65.6	51.2	99.3	82.5	87.1	73.9	102.9
1969 median income	$8,289	6,682	5,439	4,242	8,233	6,837	7,220	6,129	8,531
Number of study families	84	28	3	20	3	22	1	1	6

Source: Miriam G. Palay, Census update, City of Milwaukee, 1975 (Milwaukee: Milwaukee Urban Observatory, University of Wisconsin-Milwaukee), 1977.

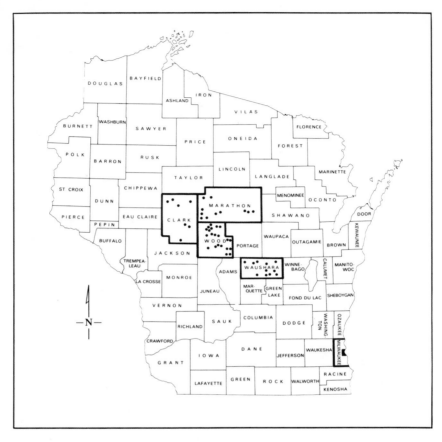

Figure 3–2. Location of Study Families in Wisconsin

Demographic Characteristics of the Sample

Some demographic background characteristics of the infants and mothers selected are presented by residence in table 3–3.

Infant

With respect to the infants' sex and birthweights, the sample is similar to national birth statistics. The sample is about evenly divided by sex, and

Table 3–2

**Population Characteristics and Summary of Health Facilities in Four
Wisconsin Counties in which Study Families Resided**

Characteristics	Wisconsin	Wood	Marathon	Clark	Waushara
Total population (1973)	4,569,000	67,200	101,616	31,273	15,480
Population per square mile (1970)	83.9	83.2	64.1	25.6	24.7
Percent nonwhite (1970)	3.6	0.5	0.2	0.3	0.3
Age distribution (1970) (percent)					
Less than 18	35.8	39.3	37.8	38.2	33.0
18–64	53.4	50.6	52.1	47.2	49.9
65 and older	10.7	10.0	10.1	14.3	17.1
Urban-rural distribution (1970) (percent)					
Rural nonfarm	23.2	36.1	32.2	47.7	67.6
Rural farm	10.9	11.7	18.2	43.2	32.2
Urban	65.9	52.2	49.6	9.1	0.3
Families in poverty (percent)	7.4	7.5	8.3	14.1	12.7
Crude birth rate (1972)	14.3	15.2	14.5	13.7	13.4
Number of general hospitals	149	2	1	1	2
Number of beds/1000 population	5.4	8.4	3.9	2.1	4.6
Number of active physicians	5,615	132	80	14	8
Rate/1000 population	1.2	1.8	0.7	0.5	0.7
Number of pediatricians	299	6	2	0	0
Number of study families within 10 miles of a hospital	110	17	5	0	4
Total number of study families	123	19	8	5	7

Sources: Wisconsin Department of Health and Social Services 1975.
Denver Research Institute 1975.
U.S. Bureau of the Census 1971.

Table 3–3
Selected Demographic Characteristics of Infants and Mothers,
by Urban-Rural Residence

Characteristics	Total		Metropolitan		Nonmetropolitan	
	N	%	N	%	N	%
Infant						
Sex						
Male	62	50.4	43	51.2	19	48.7
Female	61	49.6	41	48.8	20	51.3
Birthweight						
Less than 5 lb 8 oz	12	9.8	8	9.5	4	10.3
5 lb 8 oz–8 lb 7 oz	94	76.4	66	78.6	28	71.8
8 lb 8 oz–11 lb 1 oz	17	13.8	10	11.9	7	17.9
Mother						
Race*						
Black	58	47.2	58	69.0	0	—
White	64	52.0	25	29.8	39	100.0
Other	1	0.8	1	1.2	0	—
Poverty status						
Income less than 75% of poverty	30	24.4	21	25.0	9	23.1
Income between 75–99%	43	35.0	35	41.7	8	20.5
Income between 100–124%	13	10.6	8	9.5	5	12.8
Income 125% or greater	34	27.6	17	20.2	17	43.6
NA	3	2.4	3	3.6	0	—
Family income						
Less than $3000	16	13.0	13	15.5	3	7.7
$3–5999	53	43.1	40	47.5	13	33.3
$6–8999	24	19.5	14	16.7	10	25.7
$9000 or more	27	22.0	14	16.7	13	33.3
NA	3	2.4	3	3.6	0	—
Median income	$5,500		$5,000		$6,900	
Receiving public assistance*						
Food stamps[a]	60	48.8	52	61.9	8	20.5
AFDC/ADC[b]	64	52.0	55	65.5	9	23.1
Medicaid[c]	78	63.4	65	77.4	13	33.3
Education						
Elementary	11	8.9	7	8.3	4	10.3
Some high school	65	52.8	51	60.8	14	35.9
High school graduate	35	28.5	18	21.4	17	43.5
College	12	9.8	8	9.5	4	10.3

Table 3–3 continued.

Characteristics	Total		Metropolitan		Nonmetropolitan	
	N	%	N	%	N	%
Age						
Under 18	16	13.0	13	15.5	3	7.7
18 to 29	91	74.0	63	75.0	28	71.8
30 to 45	16	13.0	8	9.5	8	20.5
Mean age (years)	22.81		22.17		24.21	
Number of living children						
One	42	34.1	25	29.8	17	43.7
Two	36	29.3	26	30.9	10	25.6
Three	16	13.0	11	13.1	5	12.8
Four to eleven	29	23.6	22	26.2	7	17.9
Mean number of children	2.70		2.76		2.56	
Marital status*						
Single	45	36.6	43	51.2	2	5.1
Married	65	52.8	31	36.9	34	87.2
Separated, divorced	13	10.6	10	11.9	3	7.7
Household composition						
Mother, baby with or without other children	32	26.0	30	35.7	2	5.1
Mother, male partner, baby	66	53.7	35	41.7	31	79.5
Mother, baby, and extended family	19	15.4	17	20.2	2	5.1
Mother, male partner, baby, and extended family	6	4.9	2	2.4	4	10.3
Mean household size	5.17		5.27		4.95	
Total	123	100.0	84	100.0	39	100.0

[a] Data missing for 2 urban and 2 rural families.
[b] Data missing for 3 rural families.
[c] Data missing for 2 rural families.
*Urban and rural groups are statistically significantly different at $< .05$ level, Chi-square test.

about 10 percent of the infants weighed less than 5½ pounds at birth, compared to about 7 percent nationally (National Center for Health Statistics 1975).

Mother

The final sample mirrors the characteristics of low-income, inner-city residents as well as those of the rural poor. For example, in the geographic area in Milwaukee from which the urban sample was chosen, 52 percent of the population was black (Palay 1977), which compares favorably with 69 percent of the Milwaukee sample. Of the urban mothers, 25 were white, 58 were black, and 1 was American Indian. No black families lived in the sampled rural areas, a situation that accurately reflects the racial distribution in Wisconsin.

The success of the nurses in locating mothers in poverty is borne out by the figures on poverty status and family income. About 70 percent of the total sample was just at or below poverty level, as measured by the Social Security Index of income, family size, and farm or nonfarm residence (U.S. DHEW, Community Services Administration 1975). This ranged from 56 percent of the rural group to 71 percent of the urban group. Family income appears somewhat higher in the rural area, no doubt reflecting more husband-wife units in the rural area.

In urban areas, it appears that a larger proportion of the study families received public assistance. Additional computations were made, controlling on the income level. In every case, the proportion receiving Aid to Dependent Children (ADC) payments and food stamps was significantly higher in the Milwaukee group; however, approximately the same proportion of families received medicaid when the effect of income was controlled.

Examining mothers' education, there is a larger proportion of mothers who have completed high school in the rural area than the urban one (54 percent compared with 31 percent). However, in the total group about 10 percent of the mothers had only an elementary school education, and over 50 percent were high school dropouts.

Mothers were a little older on the average in the rural areas, although a larger proportion of the study babies were the only living child in the rural families. The mean number of children per family, however, did not differ significantly from the urban to rural sample. However, marital status was significantly different in these areas. Only 5 percent of the rural mothers compared with 51 percent of the urban mothers reported themselves as single. And 87 percent of the rural compared with 37 percent of the urban mothers reported themselves as married. Marital status is also reflected in the fact that 56 percent of the households have no husband or male partner present in the home. A larger proportion of metropolitan mothers are living in extended family households (23 percent), which results in a greater mean number of people in the household.

Only three background characteristics differ significantly between the rural and urban sample: racial distribution, marital status, and receipt of public assistance. These three areas reflect actual population differentials in Wisconsin's rural and urban areas.

Thus this sample of mothers of newborns who have been selected by public health nurses as exhibiting indications of incipient or actual poor-quality mothering has a diversity of characteristics.

There are women included who are black or white; live in urban and rural areas; range in age from 15 to 45; have as little education as elementary school and as much as a college degree. They are single, married, divorced, and separated. The study baby is the first birth for some, the tenth or more for others. They live in a variety of household arrangements: Some live alone with their child or children; others live with their husbands and babies; others with relatives, most often their parents.

4 Measuring Mothercraft

Introduction to Components of Mothercraft

The term *mothering* has a long and venerable place in family and child-development literature. It encompasses all the things a woman does to nurture her infant and to stimulate its growth and development.

The director of the School of Mothercraft in New York City in 1916 wrote:

> Mothercraft is the skilful [sic], practical doing of all that is involved in the nourishing and training of children, in a sympathetic, happy, religious spirit. It is not merely the care of the little baby; that is a very small, though significant, part. Its practice is not dependent upon physical parenthood, but is part of the responsibility of every woman who has to do with children as teacher, nurse, friend, or household associate. It is no more an instinct than is gardening or building. It is not merely being with children. Its requisite is vital working knowledge of the fundamental principles of biology, hygiene, economics, psychology, education, arts. It is mothering—that oldest, steadiest, most satisfactory vocation to women always and everywhere—made intelligent and efficient and joyous. (Read, p. 1–2)

Various aspects of mothercraft can be examined. Here we delineate and measure six. The first four are measured by nurses' evaluations of items in the mothercraft appraisal score (MAS). The latter two are measured by responses to questions asked of mothers.

Physical Environment

The mothercraft appraisal score includes a component on physical environment. This factor encompasses the physical home environment and concerns the condition of the home and the material objects available in the home.

Physical Treatment of the Child

A second component of the mothercraft appraisal score concerns the physical needs of the child for rest, food, clothing, and medical care.

Emotional and Cognitive Care of Child

The MAS also measures the way the mother handles the child with respect to giving warmth, affection, and stimulation.

Personality Characteristics of Mother

The MAS also evaluates certain aspects of the mother's personality that affect the physical and emotional treatment of the child.

Health Knowledge of the Mother

A certain amount of information about child care and health is important in order to perform the mothering role satisfactorily. Two ways of measuring knowledge are employed: a testing of some child-related health facts and knowledge of communicability of certain diseases. In addition, a test of knowledge of dangerous conditions for small children in the home was also used.

Attitudes toward Using the Medical System, Especially for Preventive Care

Three different attitudes of mothers were evaluated:

a. Attitudes of general skepticism toward doctors
b. Attitudes toward preventive care
c. Propensity to seek care for herself and her child with a variety of symptoms.

This chapter will describe each component of mothercraft and indicate how each was operationalized.

Mothercraft Appraisal Score (MAS)

Following the work of Norman Polansky, a set of very specific items was used to evaluate the different components of mothercraft.[1] Some of Polansky's original items were dropped because they were applicable only to a rural setting. Some items were added because they touched areas that were not represented in the original scales, for example, infant stimulation and handling by mother. At the first interview, the nurses were asked to rate the mothers on 73 specific items. After the second interview, a few items were dropped that were not clear in their meaning. The rating after the third interview included a few new items, to tap the baby's toilet training and discipline. In this analysis, only items that were rated at all three interviews are included.

In addition, a test of reliability of the items was performed using nurses and nurse supervisors exposed to the same set of activities and stimuli at the second interview. Appendix C describes the procedure used. On the basis of the results of this test, some items were dropped that did not have satisfactory interrater reliability.

The final set used in this analysis resulted in a total of 60 items. The concepts and specific items used to measure each concept follow.

Physical Environment (12 items)

The actual physical conditions of the home environment enter into the evaluation of quality of care. Specific items on housing and plumbing conditions, overcrowding, cleanliness, and faulty conditions in the home, as well as material attributes available such as bedding, furniture, toys, and books were included.

A. *Housing adequacy (4)*

1. Family lives mostly in one room in winter because of difficulty in heating entire house
2. Repairs one usually makes oneself are left undone
3. House is dilapidated; paint badly peeling, plaster broken, windows broken
4. Severe overcrowding

B. *Safety and Cleanliness (3)*

5. Gross uncleanliness in house: for example, filth, old food scraps on floor or furniture
6. Flies, rodents, bugs present
7. Only one usable exit in and out of the house

C. *Material attributes (5)*

    8. Table and chairs available to eat on
    9. Furniture is obviously in need of repair
  10. Living room doubles as bedroom
  11. Family has at least one of the following: radio, stereo, TV, or record player
  12. Child has toys of his own

Physical Needs of the Child (18 items)

A. *Cleanliness and Dress (4)*

    1. Child unwashed for long periods
    2. Child in dirty and/or ragged clothes
    3. Evidence that child's underwear (diaper) is changed as needed
    4. Child dressed inappropriately for weather

B. *Rest (4)*

    5. Child has place for sleeping at bedtime away from family living and recreation space
    6. A regular bedtime set for child
    7. Child regularly gets less than 9 hours sleep most nights
    8. Child has no routine time for arising

C. *Feeding (6)*

    9. Child fed on flexible but regular schedule
  10. Child given food appropriate to age
  11. Child fussy eater, "feeding problem"
  12. Child grossly overfed
  13. Child grossly underfed; hungry most the day
  14. Child fed meals with reasonably adequate nutrition appropriate for age

D. *Medical Care (4)*

  15. Mother refuses or resists taking child for medical care after injury
  16. Neglect of obvious medical needs
  17. Follows through on a medically prescribed treatment
  18. "Insufficient concern" to report illness to helping person

Emotional and Cognitive Care (12 items)

A. *Handling (9)*

   1. Mother occasionally "talks" or "croons" to baby
   2. Strokes or pats arm, hair, or other parts of baby's body
   3. Picks up and holds baby with relative ease
   4. Strained and tense when holding baby
   5. Uses infant seat constantly
   6. Only handles baby when necessary, for example, to change diapers, location
   7. Child is often ignored when he/she tries to get mother's attention
   8. Mother is able to show physical affection to child comfortably
   9. Child is often pushed aside when he/she shows need for love

B. *Stimulation (3)*

   10. Mother repeats "ma ma" or "da da" to child
   11. Mother teaches simple sounds by repeating: "bow wow," water, bottle, baby and so on.
   12. Mother plays with child in simple way, for example, rolls ball, grasps and pulls hands, peek-a-boo.

Personality of Mother (18 items)

Personality of the mother was tapped by items on three aspects of personality that in previous research (Polansky 1972) have shown promising relations to child neglect: dependency, apathy-futility, and verbal expression and communication with others.

A. *Dependency Scale (4)*

   1. Mother dwells on her problems with child
   2. Clings to her children
   3. Frequently refers to opinions of or quotes her mother
   4. Keeps insisting that interviewer give advice or intervene on her behalf

B. *Apathy-Futility Scale (5)*

   5. Claims that she is unable to perform at job, or housework, or get anything done
   6. Hair is usually unkept, tangled, or matted

    7. Clothes are usually dirty or in disarray
    8. From time to time becomes preoccupied or shows lapses of attention during conversation
    9. Has a sad expression or holds her body in a dejected or despondent posture

C. *Verbal Communication (9)*

  10. Speech is full of long pauses
  11. Speaks in a faint voice, or voice fades away at end of sentence
  12. Talks comfortably with interviewer by second contact
  13. Talks in an ambiguous, obscure, vague, or cryptic manner
  14. Answers questions with single words or phrases only
  15. Talks of her situation with practically no outward sign of emotion
  16. Shows warmth in voice much of time with interviewer
  17. Shows warmth in tone in discussing her children
  18. Keeps eyes closed or averted

All these items were rated by the nurse after completing each of three home visits. For each item she checked whether the activity or object was present or not present in the home or whether she had no information on which to judge. Thus there were scores for every mother taken at three points in time over the 20-month period. Following Polansky's method, only counts of negative responses were summed. That is, items were evaluated and if the response indicated a negative condition, it was given the score of -1. Thus positive responses and no information were treated the same and not counted. Mother's scores therefore reflected negative points and were assigned a negative value. The scores range from -42 to 0, -43 to 0 and -31 to 0 at the three respective waves. Mothers who are considered "good" on mothercraft therefore will have a score of 0. The larger the number of points (or negative items), the greater the negative score. The method of scoring the appraisal is shown in appendix A.

Table 4–1 shows the range, mean, standard deviation, and correlations among the appraisal scores at the three time periods. There appears to be a trend for the appraisal score to improve over time, with the greater decrease evidenced from wave 1 to wave 2. This is also reflected in the correlations among the three waves; waves 1 and 2 were most highly correlated (.704), waves 2 and 3 next (.662) followed by the longer time period between waves 1 and 3 (.501).

Components of Health Knowledge

Two measures of health-related information were obtained from the mothers. One concerned information about various aspects of baby care

Table 4–1

Appraisal Scores at Three Time Periods, Based on Sixty Common Items at Three Waves

Appraisal Score	Range	Mean	S.D.	Correlation	
				Wave 2	Wave 3
Wave 1	−42 to 0	−9.98	7.90	.704	.501
Wave 2	−43 to 0	−6.81	7.07		.662
Wave 3	−31 to 0	−6.20	7.09		

and knowledge of the communicability of certain diseases. The other was concerned with the level of awareness of unsafe conditions for a small child in the home.

Health Information (10 items)

Mothers were asked the following questions:

Q58. Please tell me whether you think the following statements are true or false

Correct Answer

A baby needs to be more warmly dressed than an adult.   (F)
It is good practice to prop a bottle so baby can feed himself.   (F)
If a baby is fat, you know he is healthy.   (F)
An overdose of aspirin is a common cause of poisoning.   (T)
Excitement can often cause a baby to spit up.   (T)
The window in a baby's room should never be opened in the winter.   (F)

Q59. Do you think one person can catch the following diseases from another?

Influenza   (yes)
Diabetes   (no)
Allergies   (no)
Measles   (yes)

An index was built from the responses, which varied from 3 to 10, with a score of 10 indicating correct information on all items. The mean score was 7.33 (*sd* = 1.68).

The first four items were repeated a year later, at the final interview. Table 4–2 shows the distribution of the mothers on this 4-point health-knowledge scale at time 1 and time 3 (17 months apart).

The nurses were permitted to discuss the items with the mother after the mother responded to the question. These figures in table 4–2 may provide some indication that the nurse's attempts at increasing health knowledge did succeed in part.

Safety Conditions in the Home

Using the work of Peters and Hoekelman (1973), a drawing was shown to the mothers which, according to the authors, demonstrated 11 conditions that were potentially unsafe (see figure 4–1).[2]

Each mother was shown the picture and was asked to point out whatever she noticed in the picture that was potentially dangerous. Mothers' answers ranged from 1 to 17 (interpolating even more problems than the authors suggested). The mean number of conditions mentioned by these mothers was 9.88 (*sd* = 2.50).

Attitudes toward the Medical System

Another aspect of mothercraft is based on various attitudes toward seeking medical care on the part of the mother. Measurements of attitudes were obtained in the structured interviews by reading series of statements to each mother that ranged from very general attitudes to specific utilization patterns. Among these are attitudes toward doctors and preventive medical care, and propensity to seek medical care for herself and her child.

Table 4–2
Health-Knowledge Score at Time 1 and Repeated at Time 3
(percent)

Health-Knowledge Score	Time 1 (N = 123)	Time 3 (N = 123)
1 Low	11	4
2	29	20
3	35	38
4 High	25	38
Total	100	100

Figure 4-1. Picture Shown to Mothers to Identify Potential Dangers
for a Child

Attitudes toward Doctors (3 items)
Three items are included in the scale to measure general skepticism toward
doctors:

> Q72. I have great faith in doctors.
> Q74. In general, I think doctors do a good job.
> Q76. In general, I think most doctors are overrated.

This score ranged from 0 to 3, depending on the number of responses
answered in a manner supportive of the doctors. It is called the
"skepticism" scale. The mean score was 2.32 (*sd* = .80).

Attitudes toward Preventive Medical Care (4 items)

The mother's attitude toward using preventive care is based on her
responses to four statements in the interview. They are:

> Q73. As long as you feel all right, there is no reason to go to a doctor.
> Q79. I would rather not go to a doctor unless I have to.
> Q80. Even if a person is not sick, he should see a doctor at least once a year
> for a routine checkup.
> Q83. How important do you think it is to take young children to a doctor
> for regular checkups even when feeling well?

The answers in a positive direction, supporting preventive care, were scored, and thus the range of scores varied from 0 to 4. The mean score was 2.61 ($sd = .99$).

The Propensity to Seek Medical Care

The inclination to seek medical care was tapped by the following two questions:

Q53. People go to see a doctor for different reasons. I'm going to describe a few medical problems and ask you how likely it is you would see a doctor if you had each of these problems. Would you say you definitely would, it's very likely you would, perhaps you would, it's not very likely or you definitely would not.

Diarrhea for about a week.
A temperature of 103° for two days.
A repeated sharp pain in your chest.
Severe cough and sore throat.
"Nerves."
Frequent insomnia (sleeplessness).
Unexplained weight loss over 10 pounds.
Allergy.
Blood in your stools.
General fatigue (always tired).

Mothers were also asked about taking their children to the doctor.

Q54a. Would you consult a doctor if the child ....

Seemed to be feeling poorly for several days and had a temperature of about 102°?
Seemed to have unexplained muscular aches or pains?
Complained of a sore throat for three days but had no temperature?
Had an earache?
Had diarrhea for a week?

These types of questions have been used a number of times in health-survey research (Mechanic and Volkart 1961; Bice and Kalimo 1972; National Center for Health Statistics 1969; Slesinger 1973b) and have indicated a correspondence between what respondents express and what their behavior is likely to be. In this research, they are termed the "propensity to seek care" for self and for baby. Each scale was scored according to the likelihood of consulting a doctor and summed over each condition. The score for "propensity to seek care for self" consisted of 10 items and was constructed to range from 10 to 50. In this sample it ranged from 18 to 50;

for baby it could have ranged from 5 to 25; and in actuality, ranged from 14 to 25. The higher the score, the more likely the mother would consult the doctor. Both for herself and her child, a sizable proportion of mothers would "likely or definitely" see a doctor for all the conditions mentioned by the interviewer: 87 percent of the mothers for baby and 40 percent for self.

Interrelationships among the Mothercraft Measures

Now let us turn to the relationships among the various measures of mothercraft. Because this research concerns mothercraft ability at the end of the period under study, the MAS at wave 3 will be examined. Table 4-3 shows the intercorrelations among the components of the MAS and with the knowledge and attitude measures.

Interrelationships among the MAS Components

Each component measure is highly correlated with the total MAS score, with the physical care of the child being the closest to 1.000. Within the components, physical care of child is most highly correlated with the physical environment (.574 at the .001 significance level), and then to the emotional handling of child (.539 at the .001 significance level). The personality of mother is most highly correlated with the physical care of the child (.494 at the .001 significance level).

Health Knowledge

Both measures of health knowledge are most highly correlated with the physical-environment component of the MAS (.287 at the .001 significance level and .254 at the .01 significance level), more than the total MAS score. Note the relatively high interrelation of health information with safety knowledge (.462 at the .001 significance level).

Attitudes

Little is significantly related to expressed attitudes about medical care, preventive care, or propensity to seek care, with the exception of attitude

Table 4-3
Pearsonian Correlation Coefficients between Components of Mothercraft

	1	2	3	4	5	6	7	8	9	10
Mothercraft Appraisal Score (MAS)										
1. Total MAS	—									
2. Physical environment	.726***	—								
3. Physical care	.849***	.574***	—							
4. Emotional and cognitive care	.783***	.464***	.539***	—						
5. Personality	.742***	.324***	.494***	.423***	—					
Health Knowledge										
6. Information	.196*	.287***	.143	.167†	.046	—				
7. Safety	.163†	.254**	.078	.096	.110	.462***	—			
Attitudes										
8. Doctors	.070	.048	.086	.001	.077	.128	.075	—		
9. Preventive care	.136	.101	.152†	.003	.161	.020	.167†	.289***	—	
10. Propensity, self	.076	.026	.084	−.075	.184*	−.117	.113	.189*	.229*	—
11. Propensity, child	.038	−.014	.094	−.069	.090	−.209*	−.059	.032	.219*	.353***

***$p \leq .001$

** $p \leq .01$

* $p \leq .05$

† $p \leq .10$

toward preventive care and the physical treatment of child (which includes 4 items on medical care) (.152 at the .05 significance level); and personality of mother and propensity to seek care for herself (.184 at the .05 significance level).

Examining the total MAS score, we see that there is a weak positive relationship with the health-knowledge items (.196 and .163, respectively, both at the .05 significance level), but no statistically significant relationship with the attitude measures.

Mothercraft Measures and Sociodemographic Characteristics

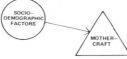

Table 4–4 shows the Pearsonian correlation coefficients among the aforementioned measures of mothercraft and the basic demographic char-

Table 4–4
Pearsonian Correlation Coefficients between Sociodemographic Characteristics and Mothercraft Measures

Mothercraft Appraisal Score (MAS)	Age	Education	Poverty	Nonwhite/ White	Rural/ Urban
1. Total MAS	.085	.321**	.195*	− .070	− .123
2. Physical environment	.054	.334***	.304***	− .131	− .176†
3. Physical treatment	.052	.254**	.170†	− .048	− .059
4. Emotional and cognitive care	.094	.221*	.022	− .039	− .083
5. Personality	.062	.211	.140	− .019	− .083
Health Knowledge					
6. Information	.312***	.307***	.158†	.260**	− .167†
7. Safety	.092	.293***	.152†	.226*	− .169†
Medical Attitudes					
8. Doctors	.201*	.106	.125	.116	− .226*
9. Preventive care	− .128	.047	.098	− .000	.001
10. Propensity, self	.085	.154†	.056	− .009	.071
11. Propensity, child	− .209*	− .092	− .092	− .252**	.354***

*** $p \le .001$
** $p \le .01$
* $p \le .05$
† $p \le .10$

acteristics of mothers. It is obvious that educational attainment is highly related to all measures, and poverty to only the total MAS score and the physical-environment component. Age and race have no relationship to the measures of mothercraft.

A number of the sociodemographic characteristics, however, are related to the measures of health knowledge, with education having the strongest relationship, and race (being white) the next. Again, little relationship is found with the attitudinal measures.

Thus we can conclude that the components of the MAS, that is, measures of the child's physical environment, physical care, emotional and cognitive care, and personality of the mother, are all contributors to the total MAS score. Health knowledge and attitudes toward doctors and the medical system are not related to the nurse's MAS rating.

Some sociodemographic characteristics appear to be related strongly to the MAS: mother's educational attainment and level of poverty. Race, rural-urban residence, and age are not.

Not unexpected is the relationship of mother's educational attainment to health knowledge. Also mothers who are older and white are more likely to have greater health information.

There are some significant relationships with propensity to take the child to the doctor. Being nonwhite and in an urban area tend to correlate with expressed attitudes toward taking the child to the doctor. The remainder of the attitudes do not appear to be related to either the MAS or sociodemographic characteristics of the mother.

Notes

1. Permission was obtained from Polansky and the Child Welfare League of America, Inc., to use some of the original items in the "Maternal Characteristics Scale" and the "Childhood Level of Living Scale" (Polansky, De Saix, and Sharlin, *Child Neglect, Understanding and Reaching the Parent,* 1972).

2. Permission was obtained from Hoekelman to use a drawing of "unsafe conditions in the home" that he used as one measure of health knowledge (personal communication, 23 September 1974).

5

Measuring the Infant's Health and Development

Three interviews were conducted with the mother during the first 20 months of the infant's life. A wealth of information about the infant's health, medical utilization, and development was obtained from the mother by the public health nurses. Chapter 5 describes the distribution on eight measures. Three of these have been selected on which to base further analysis.

Preventive Health Measures for Infant

Well-Baby Checkup Record

The following standard suggested by the American Academy of Pediatrics (Christy 1972) was used to evaluate the history of well-baby checkups obtained from the mother. The infant was scored "adequate" if

At wave 1 (3 months) the infant had received at least one general physical since leaving the hospital after birth

At wave 2 (12 months) the infant had received at least three checkups since leaving the hospital

At wave 3 (19 months) the infant had received at least four checkups since leaving the hospital

A well-checkup index score was constructed that gave 1 point for an adequate score at each of the three time periods. Thus the score ranged from 0 to 3. The mean index score for the total group over the 17-month period was 2.16, with a standard deviation of 1.08.

Table 5–1 shows the proportion of infants with adequate checkup scores at each interview, and the distribution of the infants on the index score. Values are also shown by residence of mother.

Table 5-1
Record of Well-Baby Checkups, by Residence of Mother
(percent)

Well-Baby Checkups	Total (N = 123)	Metropolitan (N = 84)	Non-metropolitan (N = 39)
Adequate at wave 1	84.6	83.3	87.2
Adequate at wave 2	66.7	72.6	53.8
Adequate at wave 3	66.7	72.6	53.8
Index Score			
0 Inadequate at all three time periods	8.9	8.3	10.3
1 Adequate at only one time period	22.8	19.0	30.8
2 Adequate at two and inadequate at one time period	9.8	8.3	12.8
3 Adequate at all three time periods	58.5	64.4	46.1
Total	100.0	100.0	100.0

Immunization Record

By the third wave, when the infant was 19 months old, the record for three immunizations was rated, using standards set by the Center for Disease Control (USDHEW 1972, 1977a,b). The immunizations and standards are as follows:

Diptheria, Pertussus, Tetanus (DPT)	The infant had three shots plus booster.
Polio	The infant had at least three doses.
Rubella	The infant had one shot.

Only 25 percent of the 19-month-old infants had three DPT shots plus the booster. However, 53 percent had the three shots but no booster; 69 percent had at least one rubella shot; and 76 percent had at least three doses of polio vaccine. With the exception of rubella, infants in Milwaukee fared slightly better than those in nonmetropolitan areas (see table 5-2).

An immunization score was constructed on the basis of the standards mentioned previously. Each satisfactory immunization was given a value of 1, resulting in a score that ranged from 0 to 3. The mean score was 2.23, with no significant difference between metropolitan and nonmetropolitan infants.

Table 5-2
Immunization Records of Infants, by Residence of Mother
(percent)

Immunization	*Total* *(N = 123)*	*Metropolitan* *(N = 84)*	*Non-* *metropolitan* *(N = 39)*
DPT (3 shots and booster)	78.0	79.8	74.4
Polio (at least 3 doses)	75.6	78.6	69.2
Rubella	69.1	69.0	68.2
Mean immunization score	2.23	2.27	2.13

Height and Weight Records

At each visit the child was weighed and measured by the nurse. Each set of measurements was coded and graphed on the NCHS Charts (1977b) and the Boston-Stuart Series (Stuart 1934). It should be noted that no standards for black infants are available, although there is some evidence that black infants are likely to be taller and lighter than white infants (Paige, Davis, and Cordano 1975; Wingerd and Schoen 1971). At birth only 15 babies weighed less than 2500 g, the accepted definition of prematurity.

The exact age of the child in months at each interview was noted, and length and weight data were plotted on the NCHS sex-specific growth charts. These charts are based on data from 867 children collected by the Fels Research Institute from 1929 to 1975 (National Center for Health Statistics 1977b). Figure 5-1 shows the distribution of the children by percentiles of weight at birth and the three time intervals at the interviews. Figure 5-2 shows percentiles for length, and figure 5-3 shows the weight for length for the three interview times. No standards are available for weight for length at birth.

Figure 5-1, weight by age, indicates that the babies are normally distributed across the percentiles, although, as mentioned previously, 15 infants (12 percent) were at or below the fifth percentile in weight at birth. This was measured by the NCHS charts as approximately 5 lb 8 oz. (It was a few ounces heavier for boys.) By the time of the first interview, only 9 babies were at or below the fifth percentile. By 12 months, there were 7, and 20 months, only 6 (5 percent of sample).

Figure 5-2, length records, indicates that at birth there were some very short and some very long babies. By the second interview (12 months), however, the extremes in length pattern were reduced, although 13 babies were still extremely short (below the fifth percentile) on length at 20 months.

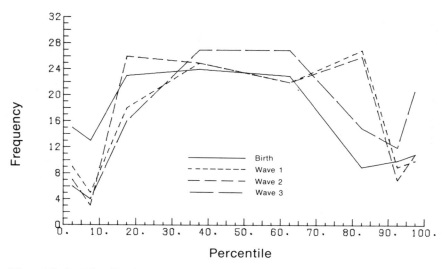

Figure 5-1. Distribution of Weight for Age, by NCHS Standard
Percentiles

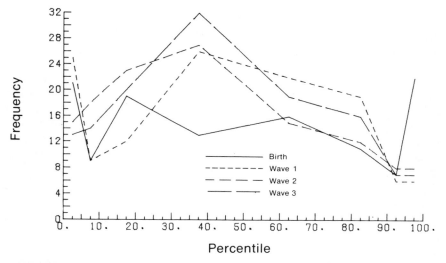

Figure 5-2. Distribution of Length for Age, by NCHS Standard
Percentiles

Figure 5-3, weight for length, demonstrates a normally distributed pattern over the entire group, with the exception of the upper percentiles. In both waves 2 and 3, there were over 35 children that were at or above the ninetieth percentile in weight for length.

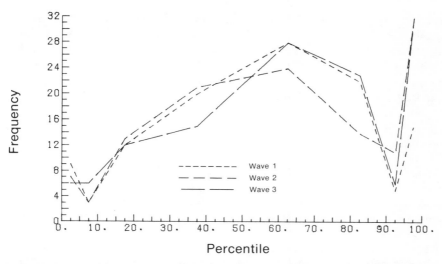

Figure 5–3. Distribution of Weight for Length, by NCHS Standard
          Percentiles

This was the only measurement that indicated a trend *away* from the normal distribution as the period from birth lengthened. These children who were at or above the ninetieth percentile in weight for length will be termed "obese" and will be examined in greater detail in chapter 7.

The charts presented here are aggregates for the total sample. Individual charts for each child were also constructed with the information obtained at each home interview plotted at the appropriate age line. Thus a graphed history exists of 123 children with respect to percentile of weight, length, and weight for length over a 19-month period from birth.

Consultation with a professor of pediatrics specializing in child development indicated that weight alone is not a reliable measure of health status with young infants because it is so variable over time and likely to reflect growth spurts. Shortness of stature, however, if not genetic and especially if a trend toward dropping below the normal range in length over time can be determined, is a sign of possible malnutrition and poor health. Weight for length is a more reliable indicator than weight but should again be considered a somewhat unstable indicator among infants, unless a trend toward obesity over time is indicated.[1]

Based on the preceding considerations, the records of all the children who fell into the extremes on each measurement (tenth percentile or below, and ninetieth percentile or above) were examined, looking for trends where the child's growth or weight record was deteriorating over time.

Outside of the sizable group who were at or above the ninetieth percentile in weight for length, no such identification could be made with length (babies who started in the normal range and later dropped to the "short" group), or weight alone (babies born in the normal range who later fell into the below normal or above normal range). Short babies turned out to be premature births, who remained small. No babies dropped into the short range who did not start out there. Therefore, only weight for length will be examined in further analyses.

Record of Baby Illnesses

At each interview the following set of seven illnesses were read to the mother, asking her at the first, second, and third interview whether the baby had experienced the illness since birth or the last interview, respectively: colds, diarrhea, diaper rash, other rash, cough, ear infection, other illness. The results were summed over the time period covered by the study. Out of a total of 21 possible illness reports, a range of 1 to 17 illnesses were reported by mothers. The mean number of illnesses reported was 8.93 for the total group. Table 5-3 shows the distribution of baby illnesses as well as the mean number reported, by residence of mother. There is little difference between the two residential areas in reported illnesses. But because there is considerable variance in number of reported illnesses, both in the metropolitan and nonmetropolitan groups, this variable will be utilized in the analysis that follows.

Record of Baby Accidents

At each interview the mother was asked whether or not the baby had had an accident. It must be noted that no definition of "accident" was provided to the mother; her interpretation of the question relative to the seriousness of the mishap and her memory of such events determined whether or not she replied in the affirmative. At the first interview, 22 mothers (17.9 percent) reported that their child had had an accident since birth; at the second interview, when the child was 12 months old, almost half the mothers reported an accident since the previous interview; and at the final interview it declined to 37 percent who reported an accident. Another way of looking at these data is to examine each mother's report over the total time period. Table 5-4 presents those mothers who reported no accident and those who reported an accident at one, two, or all three interviews.

To the author's knowledge, there are no data with which to compare these reports. Home accidents with small children rarely come to the attention of the medical professionals (and thus are not counted) unless they are serious. In data not shown here only 18 percent reported an accident from birth to 3 months; almost half the sample report an accident from 3 to 12

Table 5-3
Distribution of Total Number of Infant Illnesses, Reported by Mothers Over 20-Month Period

Number of Illnesses	Total		Metropolitan		Nonmetropolitan	
	N	%	N	%	N	%
1-4	10	8.1	6	7.1	4	10.2
5-8	43	35.0	31	36.9	12	30.8
9-12	54	43.9	39	46.5	15	38.5
13-17	16	13.0	8	9.5	8	20.5
Total	123	100.0	84	100.0	39	100.0
Mean	8.93		8.88		9.05	
Standard deviation	(3.15)		(2.95)		(3.58)	

Table 5-4
Accidents to Infant, Reported by Mother

Reported Accidents	Number	Percent
No accidents	47	38.2
Accident at one interview	38	30.9
Accident at two interviews	28	22.8
Accident at three interviews	10	8.1
Total	123	100.0

months; and 37 percent to a child 12 months to 19 months. About 4 out of 10 mothers report an accident experienced by their babies, but 3 out of 10 report two or three over the 20-month period.

The definition of an accident was left to the interpretation by the mother. A few accidents were serious such as falling off a porch and requiring stitches in the head, whereas most accidents were minor: falling and chipping a tooth; falling off a bed or high chair. No significant relationships appear between accidents and sociodemographic characteristics.

Nurse's Health Assessment

The nurse examined the infant at each home visit and noted any unusual health problems. At the final interview, however, the nurse administered a full nursing assessment—on all body systems. In addition, a health history of the child was taken from the mother that included all surgery, special tests and x-rays, accidents, hospitalizations, and communicable diseases.

Each nurse was also asked to rate the child's health as excellent, good, fair, or poor, based on all the information and observations she had gathered. Of the 123 babies, none were given an overall rating of poor health by the nurses, and only 20 (16 percent) were rated as fair. More than half the babies were rated good, and the remaining 38 (31 percent) were rated in excellent health by the nurses.

The Denver Developmental Screening Test (DDST)

At each home visit the DDST was administered to each child by the nurse. The DDST was developed by W.K. Frankenburg as a screening device for the early discovery of developmental problems in children. The test is divided into four sectors: personal-social (ability for social interaction and self-care), fine motor-adaptive (visual and manual ability), gross motor-adaptive (ability to sit, walk, and jump), and language (ability to hear, follow directions, and speak). The DDST was standardized on a sample of 1036 children aged 2 weeks to 6.4 years who reflected the racial, ethnic, and occupational group composition of the Denver, Colorado, population. Test-retest reliability over a one-week interval has been found to be 95.8 percent, and agreement between examiners ranged from 80 to 95 percent with the average of 90 percent (Frankenburg, Dodds, and Fandal 1970). A test for validity on a sample of 236 children showed high correlation of results with criterion tests: Stanford-Binet Intelligence Scale, Revised Yale Developmental Schedule, Catell Infant Intelligence Scale, and the Bayley Scale of Infants Tests (Frankenburg, Camp, and Van Natta 1971).

The DDST was a useful tool for the purposes of this research as it can be administered in the home and does not require specialized personnel to administer it. Furthermore, the nurse-interviewers in this study were familiar with this screening device and used it extensively in the Early and Periodic Screening, Diagnosis, and Treatment program (EPSDT) in Wisconsin.

The scoring of the test permits identification of "delays" in development in the four sectors, based on the age of the child. A delay may be defined as a failure to pass an item that 90 percent (or 75 percent) of children can normally pass at that age.

Using the 90-percent level of passing, at the first interview, 10 babies were classified as having delays; at the second interview 19 babies; and at the third, only 5. (One delay is not considered a significant finding. Two or more delays in one specific sector is considered a developmental delay.)

Table 5–5
Distribution of Infants by DDST Scoring at 3, 12, and 19 Months

| | Level of Passing | | | | | |
| | 3 Months | | 12 Months | | 19 Months | |
Number of Delays	90%	75%	90%	75%	90%	75%
0	113	87	104	91	118	84
1	9	28	14	21	5	22
2–4	1	8	5	11	0	17
Total	123	123	123	123	123	123

Table 5–5 displays the number of delays at each interview, for both the 90-percent level and 75-percent level.

The 18- to 20-month period is not a good one in which to test infants. Children of that age by and large are not particularly cooperative; but what is more important, it is a period in the development of the child where few skills are being learned that had not previously been tested. It is extremely difficult to fail a particular item on the test at 18 to 20 months because of the nature of the test's construction—which, of course, is based on the maturation of children at that age.

Diet of Infant

At each home interview, information was obtained from the mother on foods the infant was eating. This information is presented not only as descriptive of what a group of infants are fed but also to be evaluated as to whether the diet is adequate at each age of the study infant.

Described below are the diets of the infants when they were 3 and 20 months old. Data obtained when these children reached 12 months were not useful because too many nurses mentioned "table food" without specifying the contents of that food.

At 3 Months

At the first interview, the mothers were asked what the baby was eating and drinking. The specific type of milk offered to the baby was noted (breast, evaporated, fresh cow's milk, Similac, and so on). Mothers were also asked how often the baby was fed.

Table 5-6
Type of Milk Infant Receiving at 3 Months

Milk Type	Number	Percent
Breast milk	8	6.5
Commercial formula (such as Similac or Infamil)	82	66.7
Evaporated milk	8	6.5
Fresh cow's milk	21	17.1
Soy milk	2	1.6
Combination of two of the above	2	1.6
Total	123	100.0

Milk. All the babies were receiving milk. Table 5-6 shows the type of milk being offered.

Almost 7 out of 10 babies were receiving commercial baby formula, another 2 out of 10 either evaporated or fresh cow's milk, and less than 1 out of 10 was being breastfed.

The city public health nurses often commented on the large group of women using the commercial products. They noted that in the major city hospitals, babies were fed these preparations routinely in the hospital after birth and that mothers were sent home with sample packages to try. This started many families on the path of using this type of milk.

Vitamins. Only 31, or one fourth, of the infants were receiving a vitamin supplement at the time of the first interview.

Other Foods. Table 5-7 shows the distribution of diets of the infants with respect to intakes of cereal, fruits and/or vegetables, and meats.

Ninety-three percent (115) were receiving cereal and milk; of these, 102 also were eating fruits, vegetables, and/or meat. Five infants were consuming milk only.

Other foods such as cookies, crackers, and potato chips were noted. Only 7 out of 123 babies were fed such items. Desserts such as puddings, ice cream, and junket were also consumed.

It is generally agreed that "no nutritional or developmental advantage

Table 5-7
Diet of Infants at 3 Months

Diet	Number	Percent
Milk only	4	3.3
Milk and vitamins	1	0.8
Milk and cereal	11	8.9
Milk and cereal and vitamins	2	1.6
Milk and cereal and fruits/vegetables	33	26.8
Milk and cereal and fruits/vegetables and vitamins	12	9.8
Milk and cereal and fruits/vegetables and meat	42	34.2
Milk and cereal and fruits/vegetables and meat and vitamins	15	12.2
Milk and fruits/vegetables and meat	1	0.8
Milk and fruits/vegetables and meat and vitamins	1	0.8
Milk and fruits/vegetables	1	0.8
Total	123	100.0

will be derived from the introduction of semi-solid foods prior to the time infants are developmentally four to six months of age'' (Pipes 1977, p. 59). There is some concern currently that overfeeding during the first year of life may create obesity problems in later years. Charney et al. (1976) found that infants who attained the ninetieth percentile in weight during the first 6 months of life were over twice as likely to be overweight as adults as those who were below the ninetieth percentile. Others report no relationship between early feeding and later obesity (*Nutrition Reviews* 1977).

Obesity at 3 Months and Diet. At three months, 21 infants (17 percent) were at or above the ninetieth percentile in weight for length. The diets of these infants are compared with the remainder of the sample in table 5-8. Data were missing on weight for length for 5 infants. All of the heavy babies were receiving semisolid food, which included cereal; 86 percent also were eating fruits and vegetables and/or meat. The babies in the normal weight range were also consuming semisolid food. There appears to be little difference in type of food consumed, although no heavy babies were on milk alone or milk with fruits and vegetables.

Regularity and Frequency of Eating. About 3 out of 4 mothers reported that their infants were on a regular schedule of eating. These mothers were asked to explain the schedule. Table 5-9 shows the feeding patterns, with any bottles of milk given without other foods considered a feeding (for example, at naptime or bedtime). About one third of the infants on regular schedules ate three or four times a day and two thirds ate five times a day or more.

Of the 21 babies at the ninetieth percentile or above in weight for length at 3 months, 14 (67 percent) were on a "regular" schedule, and 8 (57 percent) of these ate five or more times a day.

Table 5-8
Diet of 3-Month-Old Infants, by Percentile of Weight for Length

Diet	< 90th Percentile		≥ 90th Percentile	
	N	%	N	%
Milk, cereal, fruits/vegetables	35	36.1	9	42.9
Milk, cereal, fruits/vegetables, meat	47	48.5	9	42.9
Milk, cereal	8	8.2	3	14.2
Milk only	4	4.1	0	
Milk, fruits/vegetables	1	1.0	0	
Milk, fruits/vegetables, meat	2	2.1	0	
Total	97	100.0	21	100.0

Table 5-9
Frequency of Feeding for Infants on "Regular" Schedules at 3 Months

Feeding Frequency	Number	Percent
Three times a day	14	15.9
Four times a day	17	19.3
Five times a day or every 4 to 5 hours	34	38.7
Six times or more a day or every 3 or 4 hours	23	26.1
Total	88	100.0

At 20 Months

Interviews held during the third wave included a 24-hour recall to obtain a record of foods eaten and eating times on the previous day. Each mention of a food was considered one portion. The foods and number of portions reported were first classified into 29 categories and then into the four basic food groups. Separate categories were created for fatty foods, sugars and sweets, and miscellaneous items. Table 5-10 shows the classification system used and the consumption frequency of the food items. The range of the number of times the food was mentioned in the 24-hour recall period is also indicated, as well as the average number of times mentioned for the group of infants as a whole.

In surveys of populations such as this one, when data are obtained during an interview, the 24-hour recall is a method that is frequently used. This method has both advantages and disadvantages and has been widely discussed in the literature (Trulson 1955; Beal 1967; Hegsted 1972; Madden, Goodman, and Guthrie 1976; *Nutrition Reviews* 1976).

The food-intake data obtained from this method are obviously not quantified nor measured precisely. In addition, the previous day's intake may or may not be representative of the usual eating pattern of individual infants. However, for a group, mean values are considered representative (Hegsted 1972). This method was used previously by the author in a study of eating patterns in which the emphasis was on usual practices rather than on specific intake of nutrients (Slesinger, McDivitt, and Moorman 1977; Slesinger, McDivitt, and O'Donnell 1980).

The frequencies reported were compared to those recommended in *Food for Fitness* (United States Department of Agriculture 1970), the guide developed for use in evaluating the adequacy of dietary intakes. The state of Wisconsin (1976) has a suggested guide for children for numbers of servings from each of the basic four groups. The total number of servings agrees with the USDA publication. Of course, the size of the servings is small for a young child (for example, 1 serving of bread equals ¼ to ½ slice; 1 serving of meat, fish or poultry equals 2 to 3 tablespoons.) the following standards for satisfactory intake were used (National Research Council, 1974; USDA 1970):

Milk	3 or more servings
Meat	2 or more servings
Fruits and vegetables	4 or more servings
Breads and cereals	4 or more servings

Four Food Groups. The average consumption as shown in table 5-10 of both milk and meats, when compared with these standards, is above the

Table 5–10
Food Intake of 20-Month-Old Infants Classified by the Four
Food Groups

| | | Number of Times Food Was Recorded in 24-hour Recall Records | |
		Range of Times	Mean Number of Times
Food Groups			
Milk	Milk Cheese Ice Cream	0–8	3.25
Meat	Meat Eggs Beans Liver Meat mixtures	0–6	2.49
Vegetables and fruits	Dark green and yellow vegetables, potatoes, and other vegetables	0–4	1.13
	Citrus and other fruits	0–4	1.02
Breads and cereals	Bread Cereal Pasta	0–7	2.85
Fats, oils	Butter, margarine Bacon Gravy Lunch meats Potato chips French fries	0–4	0.56
Sugars	Sugar, candy Sugared cereals, cookies Other sweets Kool Aid Tang Fruit drinks	0–8	1.70
Miscellaneous	Soups	0–2	0.26

accepted nutritional adequacy level, but breads and cereals fall below standard, and fruits and vegetables are considerably below the accepted level of adequacy.

Let us now turn to an evaluation of the total intake of all four food groups for each child. Table 5–11 shows the distribution of the infants

Table 5–11
Proportion of 20-Month-Old Infants Having Recommended
Intake of Four Food Groups

Score		Number	Percent
4	All four	5	4.1
3	Three	25	20.3
2	Two	54	43.9
1	One	36	29.3
0	None	3	2.4
	Total	123	100.0

fulfilling the recommended frequency of consumption of the food groups. Less than 5 percent of the infants had food from all four food groups with recommended frequency; 20 percent had the recommended number of mentions in three food groups; 44 percent in two food groups, and 32 percent in only one or *no* food groups.

This categorization of food intake is used as a measure of food adequacy at 20 months. Thus an infant may have a score of 0 through 4, which represents the number of food groups that had met the standards of USDA for adequate diets. The mean for the total group is 1.94 (*sd* = .871).

What were the foods that were most frequently lacking? Table 5–12 shows the distribution of the infants by use in recommended frequency of the four food groups. As we have just noted, only 4 percent of the children have the recommended number of mentions for all four food groups on the day of recall. Note that 10 percent satisfied *only the milk* requirement; and 17 percent *only the meat* requirement.

In addition, the proportion of children who ate *each* food group with the recommended frequency on the recall day was calculated. Table 5–13 indicates that adequate milk was consumed by two-thirds of the infants and adequate meat was consumed by 4 out of 5 infants. However, less than 20 percent had sufficient fruits and vegetables, and 30 percent breads and cereals.

Snacks, Sweets, Fats, and Oils. There were a number of foods mentioned in the child's diet that provide little nutritional value. Many of them might be classified as snack foods. These include potato chips, candy, cookies, and Kool Aid. Fatty items such as bacon and lunch meats with minimal

Table 5–12
Proportion of 20-Month-Old Infants Having Recommended Intake of Specific Combinations of Food Groups

Food Groups	Number	Percent
Milk, meat	35	28.5
Meat only	21	17.1
Milk, meat, breads and cereals	14	11.4
Milk only	12	9.8
Meat, breads and cereals	10	8.1
Milk, meat, fruits/vegetables	8	6.5
Milk, meat, fruits/vegetables, breads and cereals	5	4.1
Milk, breads and cereals	5	4.1
Meat, fruits/vegetables, breads and cereals	3	2.4
Meat, fruits/vegetables	3	2.4
Fruits/vegetables only	2	1.6
Milk, fruits/vegetables	1	0.8
Breads and cereals only	1	0.8
No food group	3	2.4
Total	123	100.0

Table 5–13
Proportion of 20-Month-Old Infants Having Recommended Intake of Each Food Group

Food Group	Number	Percent
Milk	80	65.0
Meat	99	80.5
Fruits/vegetables	22	17.9
Breads and cereals	38	30.9

nutritional value also were classified in this group. Table 5–14 shows the distribution of children by number of times these types of foods were mentioned. Approximately half the children had four or more servings of these foods, with 1 out of 5 children having six or more servings in the recall record. One fourth of this latter group were in the ninetieth or above percentile in weight for length.

Table 5-14
Frequency of Mention of Fats, Oils, and Sugars for 20-Month-Old Infants

Frequency of Mention of Fats, Oils, and Sugars	Number	Percent
0	4	3.3
1	16	13.0
2	21	17.1
3	23	18.7
4	23	18.7
5	13	10.6
6	10	8.1
7	6	4.9
8	2	1.6
9	1	0.8
10	3	2.4
11	1	0.8
Total	123	100.0

Mean number of fats, oils, and sugars per child: 3.7

Table 5-15
Frequency of Eating

Times per day	Number	Percent
2	1	0.8
3	11	8.9
4	33	26.8
5	36	29.3
6	22	17.9
7	12	9.8
8	8	6.5
Total	123	100.0
Mean		5.1

Frequency of Eating. The number of eating episodes on the recall day ranged from 2 to 8, with a mean of 5.1 (see table 5-15). Three fourths of the children had 4 to 6 eating episodes, while only 1 child ate twice during the day and 8 children had 8 meals. An eating episode represented any food intake, from a bottle of Kool Aid to a full meal.

Summary of Infant Health Measures

We have now identified six measures of child's health to be used as dependent variables in the remainder of this study. To summarize:

1. Adequacy of well-baby checkup record at 20 months
2. Adequacy of immunization record at 20 months
3. Infants who were at ninetieth or above percentile in weight for length at 20 months
4. Cumulative record of baby illnesses reported by mother over 20 months
5. Nurse's overall health assessment of infant at 20 months (excellent, good, fair)
6. Adequacy of diet of child at 20 months

We are not able to use the recording of home accidents because of inconsistency from mother to mother in reporting, nor are we able to use the Denver Developmental Screening Test because of the lack of "delays" evidenced by this group of children at 20 months.

Next let us examine the sociodemographic correlates to these six measures of infant health.

Sociodemographic Characteristics and Infant Health

Table 5-16 shows the Pearsonian correlation coefficients among the six aforementioned measures of infant's health and development and the basic demographic characteristics of mothers. We note that the infants of better-educated mothers have better immunization scores, better diets, and the nurses report their babies in better health. Poverty status is only related to one health measure: the number of baby illnesses. White mothers are more likely to feed their infants more adequate diets than nonwhite mothers. Younger mothers tend to have better checkup scores for their infants than older mothers. And finally, the more urban the residence of the mother, the better her baby's checkup score; whereas the more rural the residence, the better the nurse's evaluation of the baby's health status and the baby's diet.

Table 5–16
Pearsonian Correlation Coefficients between Sociodemographic Factors and Six Infant Health Measures

Health Measures	Socioeconomic		Demographic		
	Education	Poverty	Nonwhite/ White	Age	Rural/ Urban
Checkup score	.170†	.135	−.037	−.291**	.183*
Immunization score	.278**	.144	.020	−.034	.117
Weight for length	−.049	−.083	−.151†	.072	.160†
Illness score	−.131	−.259**	.105	−.165†	.042
Nurse's assessment	.251**	.159†	.088	.044	−.319***
Diet adequacy	.232**	.060	.275**	.117	−.279**

***$p \leq$ .001
** $p \leq$ .01
* $p \leq$ .05
† $p \leq$ .10

Relationship between Mothercraft and Infant Health Measures

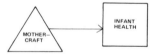

Before turning to a multivariate analysis, let us now examine the direct relationship among the various measures of mothercraft and the final measures of infant health and preventive care to be used in this analysis.

Table 5–17 displays the Pearsonian zero-order correlations among the mothercraft and infant health measures.

The MAS is significantly related at the .05 level or better to all dependent variables except the infant's number of illnesses and weight for length. Health knowledge is weakly related to only two variables: immunization score and nurse's assessment. Almost no relationship is found between expressed attitudes toward doctors, preventive care, or seeking medical care and any of the dependent variables, with two exceptions: a modest positive relationship between attitude toward preventive care and checkup score,

Table 5-17
Pearsonian Correlation Coefficients between Mothercraft and Infant Health Measures

Mothercraft Measures	Checkup Score	Immunization Score	Illness Score	Nurse's Assessment	Weight for Length	Diet Adequacy
Mothercraft Appraisal Score	.274**	.244**	-.078	.238***	-.017	.230**
Physical environment	.193*	.267**	-.103	.464***	.015	.170†
Physical treatment	.326***	.240**	-.073	.475***	-.058	.228*
Emotional and cognitive	.171†	.116	.017	.374***	-.001	.174†
Personality	.154†	.149†	-.090	.339***	.001	.142
Health Knowledge						
Information	.158†	.188*	-.083	.210*	.050	.097
Safety	.159†	.174†	.058	.189*	-.057	.049
Medical Attitudes						
Skepticism	-.133	-.149	-.118	.035	.161†	.249**
Preventive care	.181*	.056	.044	.074	.115	.021
Propensity, self	.113	.011	.017	.008	.107	.172†
Propensity, baby	.125	.082	.168†	-.111	.110	-.041

*** $p \leq .001$
** $p \leq .01$
* $p \leq .05$
† $p \leq .10$

and a stronger relationship between positive attitude toward doctors and the child's adequacy of diet.

Because the relationships, however, are very weak, inconsistent, or nonexistent between expressed attitudes and the measures of infant health, medical-attitude variables will be dropped from further multivariate analyses.

Before turning to examination of the complex relationships in the multivariate model specified in chapter 1, let us first spend a little time with some case examples of mothers and infants who were interviewed in the study.

Note

1. Consultation with Charles Schoenwetter, M.D., Associate Professor of Pediatrics, Medical School, University of Wisconsin-Madison.

Vignettes of
Selected Families

This section includes short summaries of eleven mother-child pairs taken from the 123 families interviewed.

In order to flesh out the bare bones of statistical analysis with the rich details of the complex life situations of the women in this study, short descriptions of some families are presented prior to the quantitative presentation of multivariate analyses. Relationships that are found to be statistically significant in the quantitative manipulations will be illustrated by references to the specific case material presented in this section.

These cases illustrate the interrelationship between sociodemographic and sociocultural conditions as set forth in chapter 1 and their effects on mothering and the health and medical care of the infant. Of course, the specific cases presented here were not chosen randomly from the sample, nor are they to be considered representative of all women in the sample. Fictitious names are used in all cases.

Beth and Infant Tony

Beth is a young, unmarried black woman with a ninth-grade education. She has never worked at a paid job and depends mainly on public assistance for her income. Her fear of doctors is strong, which contributes to the lack of medical care for herself and her two children. Tony, the study infant, lacks adequate emotional stimulation as well.

One of six children, Beth grew up in Kentucky and moved to Milwaukee when she was 17. Her first child, Marie, was born when Beth was 18, followed by a miscarriage eight months later. Although she had never used any form of birth control, Beth stated that she did not want another child before she became pregnant with Tony. She did not initiate prenatal care during this pregnancy until the eighth month, when she went twice to an emergency room. She was kept in the hospital for seven days after delivery due to hypertension and then did not have a postpartum checkup. Beth was 20 when Tony was born and Marie was almost 2. The three of them lived with Beth's stepsister, who was pregnant, and her 2-year old son. Tony's father, a professional boxer, did not live with them but spent time with Tony, showing a great deal of interest and emotional involvement, and he provided some financial support. Beth's income increased each year during the study, but did not rise above the poverty level until the last year. She received food stamps, AFDC, and medicaid assistance throughout the study period.

Beth reported that she did not receive regular medical care as a child and never had a well checkup, but she had appendicitis and unspecified kidney problems while growing up. Her fear of doctors stemmed from two surgery experiences, one the appendectomy and the other for an ectopic pregnancy. It is not clear when this pregnancy occurred from the interview information. She reported health problems during each of the three interviews, but had not seen a doctor since her pregnancy. At the first interview these problems were nerves, insomnia, and a kidney infection. The second time they were nerves, insomnia, and bad headaches, while at the third interview she mentioned colds, flu, upset stomach, and backaches in addition to the previous three problems. Beth had never used a birth-control method before Tony's birth. Afterward she sometimes used foam or douching and reported douching as her method at the last interview. She had never had a Pap smear. Her health knowledge was average, but she was below average on locating safety problems in a drawing of a home setting.

Beth attended church a few times a year or less. She got together with friends or relatives once a week or more until the third interview, when it dropped to a few times a year. Although Beth did not live with Tony's father, he often spent time with them and seemed genuinely interested in

Tony's welfare. The interviewing nurse felt that Beth had Tony to please him.

Tony was 2½ months old at the time of the first interview. He had received one checkup since birth, which was done in an emergency room because the public health nurse had suspected thrush at an earlier visit. Beth took Tony to the hospital to have him checked, but he did not have thrush. He had been sick with a cold and cough, which did not receive medical attention. He had not received any immunizations.

Beth's care and nurturing of Tony was below average at this point, as rated by the public health nurse. She found eleven problems, including Tony's diapers not changed when needed, lack of regular time for going to bed and getting up, neglect of medical needs, lack of follow through on medically prescribed treatment, insufficient concern to report illness, lack of verbal stimulation, housing inadequacies due to repairs that were left undone, and presence of bugs.

Beth moved three times between the first and second interviews. When the public health nurse finally located her again, she was living with a new boyfriend who was not the father of either of her children. His mother and siblings lived downstairs. Beth did not provide any information about her new boyfriend, possibly because of the involvement of the welfare agencies and her continued need for public assistance. Tony's father visited infrequently but still provided some financial support.

Beth slumped in her chair and rarely smiled during the interview, lacking the liveliness of previous contacts. She reported that she watched 11 hours of TV per day on the average.

Tony, who was now 13 months old, had received one more checkup that was obtained when Beth took him to the emergency room with a cold. He had also been in an emergency room with a scalp laceration after falling off the couch and had seen a doctor for a cough and ear infection. He had received a dose of DPT and polio immunizations, and Beth said she was going to complete the series. Tony had also been sick with diarrhea and had diaper rash. Beth reported that he usually went to bed at 3 A.M., slept until 8 A.M., and took a one-hour nap each day.

The nurse noted only five problems on the mothering appraisal form. Again, Tony lacked a regular bedtime and was getting less than nine hours of sleep. Beth continued to neglect medical needs, repairs were left undone, and the house was dilapidated.

Beth moved twice before the third interview, away from her boyfriend's apartment and then back in again, so that when the interview took place, she, Marie, and Tony were living with her boyfriend. Beth still did not talk about him, but his sister was present during the interview, and she provided the information that he was 18 years old. His mother was chronically schizophrenic and thus could not give much support to Beth. However, she was mentioned as the person Beth could go to for advice about the baby.

Previously, Beth had said she would go to a friend. Beth asked to have her blood pressure taken during the interview because of her headaches, and it was normal. She also agreed to take the children to the City Lead Clinic to check on lead poisoning and anemia, after the nurse noticed pica.

Tony was now 18 months old. He had not received any more checkups nor immunizations. He had been to an emergency room once since the second interview, with a cold and cough. He also had been sick with diarrhea and had cut his cheek in a fall from a bed. His food intake during the past 24 hours was adequate only for meat consumption, and he had only one glass of milk. His weight and length had been below the fiftieth percentile all along, and now his length was below the fifth percentile for his age. His weight for length was on the fiftieth percentile. The public health nurse assessed Tony's overall health as fair, noting his low weight, short stature, lack of immunizations, and pica with putting everything in his mouth.

Beth's mothering was very poor now; the interviewing nurse marked 19 problems on the appraisal form. Tony did not have a regular time for going to bed and getting up, and there were several problems centering around a lack of medical care. Beth often ignored Tony or pushed him away from her, and she did not play with him or provide toys. Beth seemed dejected and preoccupied, showing little emotion in her conversation and answering questions with few words. The housing was still dilapidated with unfinished repairs.

A week after the third interview the public health nurse returned to give Beth an appointment at the Lead Clinic. But Beth and the children had moved out again that morning, leaving no word on their whereabouts. Apparently, many of Beth's moves were precipitated by arguments with her boyfriend.

Beth was young, undereducated, and trying to cope with two small children. She did not have many resources to fall back on and made few plans for the future. She said she wanted to find work, doing "anything," and often seemed dejected. Beth seemed isolated, expressing this in several ways, and she had few contacts outside of her family. She had never worked and was not active in any community life. The unstable relationships with her boyfriends added to the discontinuity of her life.

The end of Tony's father's direct involvement seemed detrimental in several ways: Beth's frequent moves and the loss of his nurturing and interest in Tony's health and development. Although her poverty and lack of knowledge certainly contributed to avoidance of medical care, Beth's fear of doctors seems the strongest factor. She generally waited for a crisis point to take action. Tony had minimal health care and may have been developing a more serious problem suggested by the pica.

Cora and Infant Cindy

Cora is an older white woman who had her eleventh child, Cindy, at age 44. Cora must deal with many of the structural constraints associated with a large family and running a small farm, including poverty. Her sociocultural environment includes a close-knit family and expanding ties with the community. While at first Cindy appeared not to be getting needed attention from her mother, it was later seen that the total family environment as well as Cora's strong personal beliefs contributed to Cindy's receiving good mothering.

Cora was born into a large family in a small, rural Wisconsin town. She finished high school and then settled with her husband Ralph on a farm not far from where she was raised. When Cora was interviewed, she and Ralph had been living in the same house for more than 25 years. The dairy farm that Cora and Ralph ran did not always operate on a profit. Ralph supplemented the family income by working full time as a laborer in a local feed-mill, and before Cindy's birth, Cora was a driver for the Head Start program. Nevertheless, the family income was extremely low, always hovering around the poverty level. In the past Cora had been offended by remarks from medical professionals when her children had received medical-assistance coverage and thus made a decision to refuse to accept any form of welfare.

Cora and Ralph had their first child when Cora was 20 years old, followed by nine more births at approximately two-year intervals. During the study period the younger seven children (ages 8 through 18) were living at home and occasionally joined by an older child. It had been seven years since the birth of Cora's tenth child when Cindy, the study infant, was born. Before the pregnancy Cora was not sure whether or not she had wanted an eleventh child. When asked at each interview if she expected to have another child after Cindy, Cora first said "probably no" and then "definitely no" at the second and third interviews. Rhythm is the only form of birth control she has ever used, but in the latter two interviews, Cora said she was not using any method. At the last interview, however, Cora confided that she would mind if she again became pregnant.

Cora's ambivalence about the pregnancy and her very self-sufficient attitudes regarding health care did not adversely affect her use of prenatal health services. When she became pregnant with Cindy, Cora initiated prenatal care during the first trimester and made a total of twelve physician visits. She did not, however, return for a postpartum checkup.

Cindy was nearly 6 months old at the first interview and had received no checkups or immunizations since birth. According to Cora, "The more you run to a doctor, the more you find out something's wrong." Cora reported that Cindy had not been sick and had not even had diaper rash. Cora was somewhat concerned about her own health, reporting colds, flu, and feeling tired, but she had no plans to go to a doctor. It had been many years since Cora had received a preventive checkup for herself.

At this interview there was some question about Cora's mothering skills. She was not providing Cindy with preventive medical care nor giving the baby much attention. Additionally, Cora's emotional affect was rather flat.

Cora and Ralph have numerous responsibilities around the home, but they are also involved within their community. When Ralph returns from his job at the feed-mill, he must tend to the strict regimen of dairy farming. Yet each day he spends a little time with Cindy, and plays in a wedding band. Cora belongs to various community organizations and goes to the Catholic church regularly. However, she views her family as her primary commitment; at the first interview she emphatically denied any interest in casual friendships outside this sphere.

In responding to questions about safety and childhood illnesses, Cora demonstrated considerable knowledge about these subjects. Her opinion that use of medical services is unnecessary except for emergencies and serious illnesses does not extend to preventive measures that could be performed at home nor to dental care. Cora expressed concern about the lack of free dental care for her children and responded with interest to information regarding dental kits and fluoride tablets. She also was interested in ovulation methods for family planning.

At the second interview Cindy was 14 months old and still had not been to a doctor for any reason. Her only illness had been a cold. But Cindy's weight and length, which were within the normal range at the first interview, had dropped sharply.

Cora said regarding herself that her spirits were high most of the time and her health was excellent, although since the first interview she had had a cold. The nurse noted no health problems for Cora.

At this time Cora's mothering skills appeared very good. Her own verbal communication had improved, and she, as well as Cindy's other siblings, seemed to enjoy taking care of Cindy.

Cindy was 19 months at the final interview. She still had received no well-baby checkups or immunizations, and during the interval Cindy had been sick with a cold. However, by now her weight and length had returned to within the normal range. Cindy's nutritional status was excellent. In the 24 hours before this interview, her food intake was adequate in every food group.

Cora reported that she had no other health problems except for being sick with a cold. Her activities outside of the home had increased to include a return to her job as a Head Start driver and involvement with craft projects for the church and school. Simultaneously her nonfamilial social contacts were expanding, and she seemed stimulated by this.

At this time no problems with mothering were apparent. Cora seemed content and thriving in her relationship with Cindy. Other siblings often made Cindy the focus of their attention, but Cora maintained control over this situation "to keep Cindy from getting spoiled," she said.

While the strength of Cora's position within the family and her self-confidence in taking care of her children suggest that Cora's attitudes may have the most direct influence on the care her youngest infant receives, consideration of sociodemographic and sociocultural factors gives some indication of the source of Cora's attitudes. The combined influence of her economic circumstances, age, family size, and religious affiliation probably contributed to her early uncertainty about wanting an eleventh child. At the same time prior experience with child raising, the enthusiastic involvement of her older children with Cindy, a stable marital relationship, and a philosophy of tolerance that stemmed from these same sources may have helped Cora learn to accept and enjoy Cindy. Additionally, involvements outside the home provided new interests for Cora that may have helped her to avoid viewing Cindy as "just one more."

The poverty that Cora faces can be contrasted with that observed in some of the other vignettes in this chapter. While the family income is very low, she and Ralph have been able to maintain a high degree of continuity in their lives. Their environment—including the house, farm, and community networks—is able to reflect investments that they have made over many years. For example, the house needs repairs, but Cora's influence is evident in craft projects that decorate the interior.

Cora's attitudes regarding use of medical services appear partially linked to financial considerations. Cora said that she did not want to spend money on doctor visits unless she had to. Yet the point at which Cora perceives medical care as necessary may reflect personal beliefs as well as economic constraints. In spite of her refusal to accept public assistance, the interviewing nurse felt Cora would willingly participate in a national health insurance program. In this particular case, lack of medical care does not reflect a lack of concern, and Cindy is clearly a healthy baby.

Debby and Infant Steve

Debby is a black woman in her late thirties facing the structural constraints of little education, extreme poverty, and overcrowded living conditions. Anxiety and depression seem to dominate over expression of love, despite her concerns about being a good mother. Steve, the study infant, is not obtaining the diet, medical care, nor intellectual stimulation he needs.

Born in Mississippi, the fifth of seven children, Debby stopped school after the eighth grade. She moved to Milwaukee when she was 23. At age 24 she had her first child, followed by seven more births in two- to three-year intervals. Her fourth child died at 18 months. At the time of the first interview Debby lived with Steve, the six other children (ages 14, 11, 9, 6, 4, and 2) and her boyfriend (age 45) who was the father of all but the oldest child. Three of her school-age children are in classes for the educatable mentally retarded.

Steve was born into poverty. Debby did not report more than $2000 yearly income, an amount far below poverty, for her family at any of the three interviews. Some assistance came from ADC, medicaid and social security disability insurance. The latter was due to a disability Debby's boyfriend apparently had, although specifics are not known. Since the welfare agency was involved with the family, Debby was very reluctant to talk about him.

Debby said she had not wanted to have another child prior to Steve's birth and had used a variety of contraceptive methods. She was using foam on an irregular basis when Steve was conceived. Yet she started prenatal care in the second month, made eight physician visits and had a postpartum checkup. After Steve was born she was sterilized.

At the first interview Steve was 2 months old. He had been sick with a cold but had not been seen by a doctor nor had he received any immunizations. Debby had a history of phlebitis, and since Steve's birth, she had been sick with upset stomach, headaches, and nerves. She last saw a doctor during her postpartum checkup.

In response to questions about her feelings after the baby was born, Debby said that she often felt lonely or very remote from people, restless, bored, and very unhappy. She seemed to have difficulty expressing her own opinions and frequently compared herself to her sister, whom she saw as having "perfect children and a perfect house." For Debby, good housekeeping seemed to be the most important quality of good mothering.

Debby's first score on the mothercraft appraisal was very high, indicating a number of problems. The house needed repairs and did not have sufficient room for this large family. Steve did not have toys to play with, a regular sleeping schedule, nor adequate medical attention. Debby picked up

Steve only when necessary, did not talk or croon to him, and her voice lacked warmth. Verbal communication was poor.

Steve was 13 months old at the second interview. His only illness since the previous interview had been a cold, for which he had been to an emergency room. The interviewing nurse suspected lead poisoning. At 6 months he received a checkup but no immunizations. Debby rated her own health as poor and reported being hospitalized for nerves; details were not given.

The family environment seemed to have worsened. Debby and her boyfriend had married before the second interview, but he had since moved out. Debby seemed bitter and abrupt. She said, "Now everything is wrong, he and the kids don't get along," and she was considering a divorce.

Debby continued to rate poorly on the mothering score at the second interview. Although Steve's sleeping schedule had improved and he was being handled more, he was not eating regularly nor adequately. Other problems were the same as before, but Debby's verbal communication had deteriorated even further.

At the time of the third interview, Steve was 19 months. He had seen a doctor for an ear infection and received a physical at that time. He had also been to the doctor for diarrhea and a cold, but still had obtained no immunizations. On the suggestion made by her sister, Debby asked the interviewing nurse about Steve's right foot, which turned inwards. The nurse thought the right leg was shorter than the left.

Debby had not been to the doctor for herself since the second interview. She reported a cold during the interval, and the nurse noted high blood pressure as a chronic problem. Her husband had returned to the household by the third interview, but Debby said that her marriage was frequently upset; this was not further explained.

At this interview the mothering score contained 23 negative items. Many of the problems noted at the previous interviews persisted. Steve's diet during the 24 hours before the interview was not adequate in any food group. His intake consisted of toast with preserves and butter at 10:00 A.M., and green beans, bread, liver, a cookie, and one bottle of sugar water at 4:00 P.M. He had an intolerance for milk and drank very little of it. Other serious problems were neglect of medical care, no sleep schedule, and poor stimulation for Steve; Debby was apathetic and communicated poorly both with her children and adults.

During the year-and-a-half observation period, continued poverty was the most obvious structural constraint. Although Debby was often cleaning the home's interior when the nurse arrived, the house was dilapidated and overcrowded with eight to nine family members. The full extent to which lack of money contributed to Debby's problems is not known. She felt uncomfortable with professionals of any kind and relationships with welfare agencies may have added pressures to the domestic situation.

At the sociocultural level, Debby depended on her sister and husband for her main sources of social support. They seemed to influence the medical care her children received. Debby noted her sister's observation of Steve's orthopedic problem and followed her example in taking the children to a clinic for lead poisoning. At the same time Debby's admiration for her sister seemed related to her own negative self-image. Debby's husband initiated medical care for the children more often than Debby did, but their relationship was not stable. At the conclusion of the third interview, the nurse was not visiting Debby as frequently as before because Debby did not follow through on her suggestions.

What seemed to predominate in Debby's relationship with her children was the continued absence of positive actions and emotions rather than overtly negative ones. Although Steve was an unwanted baby, she obtained prenatal care. She did take Steve to the doctor on a few occasions, and questions arise why immunizations were not initiated at those times. With the exception of the sugar water, none of Steve's foods on the day before the third interview would be considered bad for him; he needed other types of food, for example fruits, grains, and milk products. The nurse noted in a number of places that Debby loves her children and has good intentions but that "emotional stimulation is above and beyond anything she had known."

Ellen and Infant Susan

Ellen is a 31 year old white woman living in Milwaukee with her husband, Bill, her mother, and her daughter Susan, the study infant. The family income is quite adequate as Bill is employed full time as a welder. Family life is very smooth with Ellen running a clean, well-ordered household. Susan receives necessary medical care, and she seems to be a healthy, thriving child.

Ellen grew up in Milwaukee with her three older brothers, completing high school there. She later worked as a packer and inspector at a cash-register-manufacturing company. She recalled that she had regular medical care as a child, due mainly to the fact that she was often sick and was hospitalized for pneumonia almost yearly.

Susan is Ellen's first child, and she definitely was a wanted baby. Ellen had been using the pill but stopped some time prior to the pregnancy and then continued to use it throughout the duration of the study. She planned to have a second child when Susan was three years old. Ellen obtained regular prenatal care while pregnant, starting in the third month, and also had a postpartum exam. Her mother, who was 69 years old, moved in shortly after Susan's birth because her husband had died recently. She provides some advice and help with the baby's care, but Ellen emphasized her husband's assistance more, praising his willingness to care for Susan and help with the housework.

Ellen was very conscientious about having a good home for her family, and she had a strong liking for orderliness. Her home was always very clean, neat, and nicely decorated with family pictures. However, she seemed to be only moderately integrated into the community. She did not work or plan to return to work after Susan was born. She attended church two or three times a month, but did not go out to any club meetings and rarely went out to eat, drink, or see a movie. She visited friends and relatives two or three times a month, mentioning a brother and step-sister as two people she could call on for help or advice about Susan.

Ellen kept meticulous records of the family health-care history and also had notes on Susan's feedings while she was an infant. Ellen had not been to a doctor for a general checkup for over 10 years but had received regular dental care, as well as her prenatal care and regular Pap tests. The only illnesses she mentioned for herself during the entire study period were a cold and the flu, but she did not see a doctor for either of these. She had a brief hospital stay when Susan was a year old for surgery on a deviated septum, after having bad sinus infections.

Susan was 2½ months old when the first interview took place. She had received one checkup since coming home from the hospital, and had started DPT and polio immunizations. She had not been sick since birth but was given syrup to prevent colic. She was on regular schedules for eating and sleeping, going to bed at 9 P.M. and waking at 7:30 A.M.

Ellen's care and mothering of Susan was rated as excellent by the interviewing nurse. She noted that Susan tended to be a fussy eater, possibly due to the colic problem.

Susan was almost 12 months old at the second interview. Ellen's mother was not living with the family at that time because she was visiting each of her children, and would be away for several months. Otherwise, the family situation continued as before. Ellen was playing soft religious music on the stereo during the interview, and the public health nurse said she got a general feeling of religiousness from Ellen. Susan was limited to playing in the kitchen and living room as Ellen kept the other rooms closed. She verbally disciplined Susan in a firm, soft voice, and Susan did not try to play with the photos and nick-nacks decorating the home. There were no toys available during the interview, but Ellen said she has some. The family was planning to build a house in a suburb of Milwaukee soon.

Susan had received two more checkups and another series in the DPT and polio immunizations. She had been sick with a cold and cough, and diaper rash, and had seen a doctor for diarrhea and upset stomach. She regularly slept 11 hours a night and took a 3-hour nap every day.

Ellen had no problems with mothering, as rated by the interviewing nurse.

Between the second and third interview the family moved into their new suburban home. Ellen's mother had not yet returned from her visits to her other children. At the third interview Susan was 20 months old. She was a curious and active child. She had received three more checkups as well as the final dose of DPT and polio immunizations, and the rubella and mumps immunizations. She had been to an emergency room once for X-rays where Ellen's suspicions of croup were confirmed, and had also been sick with a cold and diaper rash. Ellen mentioned one accident in which Susan fell down six steps and bloodied her nose. Susan's food intake during the 24 hours prior to the interview was adequate in three food groups (milk, meat, fruits/vegetables) and inadequate in the bread-cereal group because she had only two servings of bread that day. Her weight had consistently remained near the fiftieth percentile from birth, but her length shot up to over the ninety-fifth percentile at 20 months. However, her weight-for-length was still above the tenth percentile.

As with the second interview, Ellen's mothering presented no problems.

Ellen is somewhat older and more mature than many new mothers and additionally is in a financially secure position. As a result she has very little difficulty in handling the new demands of an infant in the family. Although some more "settled" couples may have problems in changing their life-style when a baby is born, Susan was wanted and perhaps had been anticipated for some time.

Ellen and Bill seem to have a strong mutually supportive relationship in which their respective roles are clear. Ellen enjoys both her child and her husband. She knows when to seek medical care and realizes the importance of preventive care for her daughter. Susan had very few illnesses as an infant, none serious, and as a result of being completely immunized, she is much less at risk than many children of her age.

The outcomes for this family look very good. A second child is wanted and seems as though it would not present any problems. Susan is thriving in her environment with no serious problems.

Linda and Infant Robert

Linda is an unmarried black woman with two children. She is poor and undereducated, providing little health care for her children. Perhaps more significant, she is very carefree and unconcerned about providing a sense of continuity in their lives. She seems to live as she pleases, often behaving as though she does not have any children, which makes intervention by social-service workers very difficult and leaves the future of her children open to many potential problems.

Linda was born in Chicago, one of three girls, and had lived in Milwaukee since she was 12. She did not finish high school and never married. Her first child, Jane, was born when she was 17, followed just five and one half months later by a stillbirth. There may have been a miscarriage two years later, but Linda did not seem positive of this. She never used any form of birth control, saying she did not mind if she became pregnant. Her second child, Bobby, the study baby, was born when she was 29. She obtained regular prenatal care starting in the third month but did not have a postpartum checkup.

Linda's health knowledge was slightly below average. She received little medical care aside from prenatal care, claiming that she was never sick. During her first interview colds and insomnia were her only health problems, and colds were the only problem at the second interview. Linda was 8 months pregnant when the third interview took place, and she was seeing a doctor regularly for prenatal care. She had been bothered by colds, upset stomach, and nerves in the time between the second and third interviews. Linda said she receives regular dental care, possibly because she has a partial upper denture for her front teeth that she does not wear all the time.

Linda worked in a factory until her pregnancy with Bobby, running a machine making plastic knobs for stoves. She did not go back to work during the duration of the study but said she planned to return to the factory later on, not saying exactly when. She received food stamps, ADC, and medicaid assistance throughout the study, and her income was below poverty level except for the second wave, when the weekly value of her assistance check was slightly above poverty level.

Several of her relatives also lived in Milwaukee, including her mother, and an aunt lived downstairs. Although she did not mention any brothers when asked about siblings during the first interview, later in the study she mentioned a brother living in Milwaukee. Her aunt was a source of advice about the baby. Linda's 12-year-old daughter helped care for Bobby every day. She visited her relatives and friends frequently each week and went out more than once a week. She did not go to church more than a few times a year and did not belong to any clubs. Her daily routine, described during the first interview, was to get up at 5 A.M., do all the housework by 9 A.M., and then watch TV until 3 P.M. She often spent this time on the phone with a friend while they watched the same TV show—usually soap operas.

Linda's home was dark because the shades were all pulled down, and the kitchen was very sparsely furnished. There were four beds in the apartment, but Linda was uncommunicative about whether anyone else lived with her and the children. She had very little eye contact with the interviewing nurse during the first visit, looking mostly at the activity on the street outside her kitchen window, and her conversation jumped quickly from one subject to another. She seemed energetic and quick tempered. For example, the public health nurse related that she made an appointment for Linda to go to the city clinic. She arrived at the wrong building at the wrong time, became very enraged when she could not be seen, and said she would go to Children's hospital instead.

Bobby was 2½ months old at the time of the first interview. He had received one checkup since coming home from the hospital but no immunizations. He had a cough and cold before the first interview, which might have prompted the visit to the doctor. Linda reported that Bobby has a regular sleeping schedule, going to bed at 7 P.M. and waking up at 5 A.M., sleeping in her bed.

Linda's mothering was rated as poor by the public health nurse, who listed 12 problems on the mothercraft appraisal score. Four of these problems concerned the physical environment, including lack of toys for Bobby. Linda did not talk or play with Bobby, and she did not show him much physical affection. He lacked a regular schedule. Linda's lapses of attention and averted eyes during the interview were also noted.

Linda and the children moved before the second interview, and the nurse made four attempts before she found Linda at home. Bobby was not there, however. He was staying at Linda's brother's house because she did not have any food at home. Linda reported that he often stays there on weekends, also, apparently because of lack of food and Linda's desire to be able to go out whenever she wants to. The interviewing nurse visited Linda's brother so she could measure and test Bobby. Linda's mother was there and reconfirmed the fact that Linda would leave Bobby in anybody's home and take off as she pleased. Linda had not mentioned the children's fathers or any boyfriends, except to say that Bobby's father lived in Florida.

During the second interview Linda described some of Bobby's recent antics such as throwing objects into the toilet and bathtub, playing with the stereo set, pulling the nightlight out of its socket, and tearing magazines. She said that Bobby had been sleeping with her, and now that she was trying to get him to sleep in his own bed, he would crawl in with her or with Jane and bite them. She generally is amused by his mischievous behavior, giggling while talking about him.

Bobby was 13 months old when the second interview took place. He had received only one more checkup, which was not enough to be rated adequate, and still had not been immunized at all. Linda reported that he had had colds, diarrhea, ear infection, diaper rash, and prickly heat rash, had seen a doctor in Children's Hospital twice, and had the checkup on one of these visits. Linda said he had a cold and diaper rash all the time. He was now sleeping from 10 P.M. to 8 A.M. with a 3- to 4-hour nap in addition. He did not have an eating schedule but ate snacks all day.

Linda now watched about 12 hours of TV each day, and mentioned reading several magazines such as *True Romance*. She had never used contraceptives but was hoping she would not get pregnant again since there had been a 12-year lag between her two pregnancies.

Linda's mothering ability was somewhat better this time, as rated by the public health nurse. There were three problems with the physical environment, including the lack of toys, and three more related to Bobby's lack of regular schedules. But the problems noted before in Linda's affect were not mentioned. However, there were many unanswered items because Bobby was not there and the nurse could not observe Linda's interactions with him.

The family moved again before the third interview, and the nurse made three visits before finding Linda at home. When the nurse arrived, Linda surprised her by being naked and pregnant when she answered the door. She then ran to put some clothes on. Linda seemed relaxed and unconcerned about her pregnancy. She was getting prenatal care and taking vitamins and iron. She said she had wanted another child, contradicting things she had said earlier, but that this pregnancy came too soon. She definitely did not expect to have any more children after this one, but did not mention plans for contraception.

Bobby was not at home again and continued to spend time at his grandmother's house and with other relatives, often being fed by them. Linda had new stories to tell the nurse about his mischievous behavior, including throwing a spoon into his grandmother's toilet so that it overflowed into the apartment below hers. Linda laughed heartily at this. She was also unconcerned about Bobby's vocabulary, which consisted of mama, dada, baby, and fucker. Jane, who was now 13, often stayed with relatives so she could go to a school that she preferred to the one in her mother's neighborhood. But Linda kept her at home to watch Bobby at times.

Linda now said that Bobby's father was in Detroit, and the father of her expected child was also from out of town and did not know that she was pregnant. Because Bobby was not at home when the nurse took the third interview, she returned several weeks later to see him. Linda had delivered a healthy boy after being out of town for three days, getting home just in time to get to the hospital. Jane was now caring for both of her young brothers when her mother was out. Linda's mother had moved to a northern suburb of Milwaukee and no longer took care of Bobby, so it seemed that more of the burden had fallen on Jane.

Bobby was 19 months old when the third interview took place. Linda reported that he had not had any immunizations yet nor any more checkups. She said she did not know where the city immunization clinics were. Bobby had a cold, diarrhea, diaper rash, and an ear infection between the second and third interviews but had not been to see a doctor. His diet as reported in a 24-hour recall was adequate in milk and meat; he had no fruits at all during that day, but Linda may not have known about his intake at his grandmother's house. His length had been consistently below the twenty-fifth percentile all along, but his weight fluctuated, up to the ninetieth percentile at 13 months. When the nurse finally got to see him, his weight had dropped to below the seventy-fifth percentile, so his weight-for-length was on the ninetieth percentile instead of above the ninety-fifth percentile as it was before.

Linda's mothering ability was rated poorly by the interviewing nurse, similar to the first interview. The house was dilapidated, and repairs were undone. Bobby had no sleeping or eating schedules, his medical care was neglected, and Linda did not play with or verbally stimulate him.

Overall, the fact that Linda's income is below the poverty level does not seem as important in this case as in some of the others. She obtains some medical and dental care for herself and Bobby, and does not feel that she is neglectful of his medical needs such as immunizations. Although she does have problems in keeping enough food in the house to feed the children, this is not clearly related to her poverty status. It seems more a case of not planning well and being able to rely on her relatives as long-term babysitters whenever she is unwilling to care for her children.

Linda seems to have an active social life, judging from the frequency with which she leaves the children with her relatives. She goes out of town during some of these times, although her relationships with men and with the fathers of her children were never described openly. Aside from seeing her relatives frequently, she is not well integrated into her community in any conventional sense.

The lack of continuity and stability for the children may present some problems as they grow older, but Linda does not see anything wrong with her life-style. She is happy and carefree and feels that her children are being raised in a good way. She is not able to discipline Bobby to a great degree but feels that his behavior is normal and is not worried about future implications of her actions.

Marcia and Infant Jeremy

Marcia is a young black woman who at age 18 was confronted with being a teenage mother. Her income is low, she is single, and there is no evidence of any relationship with Jeremy's father. Although Jeremy received adequate medical care throughout the observation period, at the beginning Marcia's mothering skills were not good. However, through the year and a half that followed, Marcia's mothering skills showed consistent improvement. It is not possible to identify which of the many factors in Marcia's structural or sociocultural environment are responsible for this change. By the last interview Jeremy's needs are apparently being met through Marcia's ability to cope with a difficult situation and her extended family's involvement with Jeremy.

Marcia has lived in Milwaukee most of her life. She is the second born and oldest daughter of her mother's six children. Marcia lived with her baby and four teenage siblings (ages 16, 15, 14, and 13) in their mother's home when first interviewed. In addition, her 16-year-old sister, April, had two children (ages 2 and 10 months) who were also in the home. This household composition remained stable at all interviews with the exception that Marcia's youngest brother (age 13) no longer lived with them at the third interview. At no time was any reference made to Jeremy's father, Marcia's father, or the father of April's children. It is clear that none of the men were in the home.

Jeremy is Marcia's first and only child. Before becoming pregnant, she had graduated from high school and gone to work as a secretary. Prior to her pregnancy Marcia had wanted children at some time, but she said that this pregnancy was sooner than she wanted. Although she was using no method of birth control when Jeremy was conceived, at the second and third interviews she reported using the pill; she said it would be eight years or more before having another child.

Marcia continued her secretarial work into the ninth month of pregnancy. She was somewhat late in initiating prenatal care, waiting until the fourth month to make a first physician visit. However, she followed through with nine additional appointments and a postpartum checkup. By the first interview, when Jeremy was 3 months old, Marcia had returned to her job and worked daily until 2:30 P.M. Jeremy was taken care of by cousins or nephews while she was at her job. Marcia's net income was less than $3000, below the poverty level for a woman and her child. Medicaid and ADC gave Marcia and Jeremy some assistance.

Jeremy had diarrhea, diaper rash, and colds during his first three months. But his DPT and polio immunization series had been started, and he had received a well-baby checkup. At this first interview Marcia appeared tired. She said that since Jeremy's birth, she had acquired a urinary infection, could not sleep well at nights, and had been sick with a cold.

Marcia's first interview mothercraft appraisal score was not good. Although Jeremy was receiving some of the physical and medical care he needed, he was not being fed regularly, and Marcia's emotional attitude toward him was questionable. She was despondent during the interview and had trouble focusing her attention on much of anything, including her baby. Thus Jeremy was not receiving spontaneous physical affection nor various forms of stimulation from his mother.

Jeremy was 14 months old when the second interview was held. He continued to obtain recommended medical care with four well-baby checkups and followup on his DPT and polio immunizations. However, he had several illnesses, including diarrhea, diaper rash, colds, a cough, and an ear infection; Jeremy was seen by a doctor for the latter three. Marcia had also been to the doctor for a urinary-tract infection and a cold. She viewed her overall health as good, but reported that she had recently had upset stomach, headaches, and insomnia.

Since the previous interview, time Marcia spent in activities outside the home had increased. She had begun attending morning classes at a local technical college and acquired a full-time job as a counselor's aide. She finished work at 8:30 P.M. and afterwards often went to the library to study. Her income increased by about $25 a week, but she still bordered poverty and received medicaid, ADC, and food stamps.

Some tension was apparent between Marcia and her mother at this interview. Because of work and school Marcia had little time to be with Jeremy. An aunt and her mother were now assuming responsibility for the baby while she was away from home, and Marcia's mother did not seem happy to have another baby to care for. These feelings, however, did not appear to interfere with the way Jeremy's grandmother treated him.

Marcia's mothercraft score improved at this time. Although she was talking and playing more with Jeremy, Marcia's emotional handling of Jeremy and her own self-expression were still poor.

When Marcia was next interviewed, Jeremy was 19 months old. The interviewing nurse rated his overall health as good. He had been sick with many of the same problems as in the preceding interval, but his length and weight were within the normal range and his immunizations were complete with the exception of a booster. Jeremy's diet, based on the previous day's intake, was deficient only in fruits and vegetables. Marcia had been sick with upset stomach and colds, but no longer complained of insomnia and headaches.

At the final interview, Marcia's mothercraft assessment was close to perfect. While she was not spending any more time at home than before, during her time with Jeremy she was alert, spoke warmly of the baby and fondled him affectionately. It is not obvious what caused this change in Marcia by the third interview, although improvements in her mothering skill were also demonstrated between the first and second interviews. It is clear, however, that Marcia's ability or willingness to express herself was associated with the manner in which she demonstrated affection toward Jeremy.

Structural constraints such as poverty can be understood only in Marcia and Jeremy's case with more information on the family. While Marcia's income always hovered around poverty, the kinds of reciprocal financial arrangements with the kinship network are not known. Marcia's age, her educational status, and work experience may interact in complex ways with her mothering. Having a baby did not prevent Marcia from pursuing some of her personal goals nor isolate her from activities outside the home. She continued her education beyond high school, worked, belonged to organizations, regularly read newspapers, and went out to eat, drink, or see movies at least once a week. But these activities also kept her away from Jeremy and may have contributed to her early lack of emotional involvement with him. It is not clear who took responsibility for Jeremy's preventive medical care, which was always satisfactory.

Neither is it possible to know the impact on Jeremy and Marcia of the family situation into which Jeremy was born. The emotional climate in the home, the grandmother's apprehensiveness about Jeremy and her relationship with Marcia were undoubtedly influenced by prior experience with her daughter April (who was only 14 or 15 when her first child was born) and April's children. But many relatives outside the home along with Jeremy's grandmother provided love and child care for Marica's baby when Marcia could not.

No simple formula for coping with teenage pregnancy emerges from Marcia's case. However, it seems apparent that background and sociocultural factors made a difference. Perhaps the way Marcia dealt with her family, work, and school influenced the way she felt about herself. Marcia had difficulties at first, but she learned how to give Jeremy the love he needed. Simultaneously she became less bothered by symptoms of insomnia and bad headaches.

Sandra and Infant Michelle

Sandra is a young black woman with four small children, living in Milwaukee. She is poor, a high school dropout, and has never married. Although she has good intentions, her children are not receiving adequate medical care, and Sandra seems depressed. She is overwhelmed by the demands of her family.

Sandra was born in the Milwaukee area and grew up there with her six siblings. She worked at a variety of jobs after leaving high school, including being a waitress, sales clerk, and bartender. Her first child, James, was born when she was 18, followed a year later by Charlene, and then a year and a half later by Todd, when she was 21. Sandra then had two abortions, followed by the birth of Michelle, when she was 25. Sandra started prenatal care for this pregnancy in the second month, and then had a tubal ligation after Michelle was born, but she did not get a postpartum checkup. Sandra said she had wanted another child, but that the last pregnancy came sooner than she really wanted.

Sandra lived alone with her four children throughout the study. Her mother was dead, but she saw other relatives frequently, usually more than once a week. She went to church only a few times a year, and did not belong to any organizations. Sandra started working full time on a packing line at a chocolate company when Michelle was about a year old, but kept the job less than one year. Her income stayed below poverty level throughout the study, and she received food stamps, ADC, and medicaid assistance all along. She had a few woman friends whom she could ask for advice about the baby, but always seemed glad to have the public health nurse come to visit. Sandra went out to eat, drink, or see a movie once a week or more. She never provided any information about the father or fathers of her children, or about any boyfriends.

Sandra had not had much contact with the public health nurses before and needed assistance in setting priorities for herself and the children. She was receptive to suggestions about obtaining preventive medical care for her children. Sandra was harsh with her children when they interrupted the interview and at times seemed overwhelmed by the tasks facing her, unable to enjoy her children.

Michelle was 3½ months old when the first interview took place. She had not had a checkup or any immunizations. Although Michelle had several illnesses during the first three months, including diarrhea, a viral rash, and a cough, her only medical care was a visit to the emergency room when she had her first cold. She was on a regular schedule for eating and sleeping, going to bed at 8:30 P.M. and waking at 8:30 A.M.

Sandra had not received a general physical exam for several years, outside of her prenatal care, but had seen a dentist recently. She had problems with a cold, upset stomach, and bad headaches during the three months preceding the interview. Her health knowledge was poor, and she scored below average on an item that required her to locate home safety problems shown in a drawing.

The interviewing nurse found 9 problems in Sandra's mothering when rating her on the mothercraft appraisal score. Michelle's clothes were dirty, her diapers were not changed as often as needed, and her food intake was not appropriate as it included too many solid foods for her age. Sandra did not talk to Michelle, repeat sounds to her, or play with her. And the home lacked a table and chairs for eating together.

Sandra had started working at the chocolate factory before the second interview. She left the children with a babysitter while at work. During the second interview the older children seemed to crave affection from their mother but she paid more attention to Michelle than to the others. The family had moved four times since the first interview, now living in a large flat that was sparsely furnished.

The public health nurse had visited the family three times between the first and second interviews, giving Sandra information on nutrition and child development, and encouraging her to seek medical care for the children. Michelle had no immunizations and an umbilical hernia; Charlene had an unevaluated hernia and an enlarged tonsil; Todd had not received adequate medical care or immunizations; and James also had a hernia. Sandra had a cold and problems with nerves, but had not been to a doctor since Michelle was born.

Michelle was 13 months old when the second interview took place. She still had not received any immunizations or checkups. She had been seen by a doctor in an emergency room when she had a cold and flu but had not been to a doctor when she had diarrhea and diaper rash. She continued on regular eating and sleeping schedules, getting 11 hours of sleep each night with a 1½-hour daytime nap.

Sandra's mothering, as rated by the public health nurse, had changed and became slightly worse than at the first interview. Michelle's diapers were not changed as needed, she did not have toys of her own, and Sandra still did not talk to her enough or play with her. Sandra neglected dental needs and preventive care and did not take her children for medical care when they were ill. Repairs around the apartment were not done, and there were bugs present. Sandra felt apathetic, not able to get things done, and at times she would dwell on her problems with the children.

When the third interview took place, Sandra's situation had deteriorated. She was depressed and poorly motivated, letting James (who was now 8) take care of Michelle and spending little time with the children herself. Michelle even called James "mama" at times. Sandra met the children's most basic needs for food and clothing but paid very little attention to their other needs such as verbal stimulation and affection. Medical care continued to be ignored. Although Sandra stated that she "always sees the doctor," she later said she felt guilty about never getting medical care for her children.

The apartment was dark and dingy. Sandra tried to keep the older children out of the room while the interview went on, but when they came in, she expected them to be quiet. She demanded an immediate response to her disciplinary efforts, seeming intolerant of the children's behavior. She seldom read or talked to the children. The interviewing nurse tried to help Sandra set some realistic goals for health care, which were to get care for herself as the sole adult, to get James's hernia corrected, and to get preventive care, including lead-poisoning checks, for all the children.

Sandra had been to a doctor with a virus after the second interview. But she also had complaints of bad headaches, nerves, chest pain, shortness of breath, and possible anemia, none of which had been brought to the attention of a doctor. She rated her own general health as fair, and said the same for Michelle's health.

Michelle was almost 20 months old when the third and last interview took place. She had not been seen by a doctor at all since the second interview, although she had a cold and cough at one point. Her food intake during the 24 hours prior to the interview was adequate for meats and grains but included no fruits or vegetables and only one portion of milk. Her weight and length had been between the fiftieth and ninetieth percentiles all along, but her weight-for-length improved from the tenth percentile at 3 months to slightly above the fiftieth percentile at both 13 and 20 months of age. She continued to get 12 hours of sleep each night plus a 2- or 3-hour nap. The public health nurse rated Michelle's overall health as fair, noting the lack of both immunizations and attention to the hernia.

Sandra's mothering was very poor this time, as rated by the nurse who found 23 problems. The apartment was dilapidated, with repairs undone. Sandra neglected medical care, and did not follow through on medically prescribed treatment. Michelle had no regular schedule for eating and sleeping, and received little verbal stimulation from her mother.

Sandra faces a number of serious problems in trying to cope with her family. At the age of 27 she has four children aged 8 and under, while living on a limited income derived from public assistance. In addition, her limited educational background has not equipped her to understand child development or the need for preventive health care. She rarely talks with or reads to her children, omitting much of the stimulation necessary to their development.

Sandra is basically alone with her children, having never married nor established a long-term relationship with a male partner. Her relatives appear to offer little tangible support and her involvement in the community is minimal. The public health nurse provided information and suggestions in a variety of areas, but Sandra was not capable of incorporating new ways into her life-style without the necessary support of others.

The lack of preventive care for Michelle and her siblings is cause for concern, as well as the lack of attention to existing problems such as the hernias. It does not appear that the care Michelle is getting will improve at all as she grows older. Indeed, Sandra's increasing depression and apathy points to continuing neglect of both medical and developmental needs of the children.

Sue and Infant Todd

Sue is an 18-year-old white mother of two boys, who lives with her husband and children in a trailer home in rural central Wisconsin. Sue lacks confidence in herself, and her husband seems to dominate their relationship. Todd, the study infant, received very little health care, due to both the family poverty and Sue's limited knowledge of health.

Sue was born in a town in rural Wisconsin, one of nine children, and had lived in the area all her life. She never completed high school, although John, her husband, was a high school graduate. Their first son, Gene, was born when Sue was 15, and Todd was born just after her eighteenth birthday. John was 22 years old.

Sue had used several methods of birth control, including the pill, but stopped before becoming pregnant with Todd. Sue said she had wanted another child and started prenatal care in the first trimester. She also had a postpartum checkup.

John ran a local trucking company that hauled grain and hay for the surrounding farmers. Although he worked very hard, the family income was far below poverty level at all three interviews. John and Sue refused to accept any public assistance, saying they were "too proud" for welfare. They did allow the county family-planning service to pay for IUD insertion after Todd's birth. Sue continued to use the IUD throughout the duration of the study. She wanted to have two more children but planned to wait two to four years. She said she would not have any more children until they moved out of the trailer and into a house.

Sue has never worked and seemed somewhat isolated from social contacts. She never went to church or any clubs and saw friends or relatives two to three times a month. At the last interview this changed to "a few times a year." But she did mention her mother and mother-in-law as the people she would call on for help or advice with the children. The interviewing nurse had known Sue for two years before the study began. In the beginning Sue was threatened, talked very little, and did not follow the nurse's recommendations. But when the study began, the nurse felt they had a trusting relationship: Sue was open about the family's financial problems and marital difficulties. She accepted advice about nutrition, child care, housekeeping, and communication skills. Although Sue had some misunderstandings about medical problems and causes, she seemed to be learning more from the public health nurse.

Todd was 5 months old when the first interview took place. He had been to the doctor for one checkup but had not received any immunizations. He had been sick with German measles, cold, cough, ear infection, and diarrhea. His sleep schedule was to go to bed at midnight and wake at 8:30 A.M.

Sue had not had an asymptomatic checkup for several years, and had not been to a dentist for 10 years. She recently went to the doctor because of a feeling of weakness and abdominal burning that was not diagnosed. She had also been sick with a sore throat and had problems with nerves.

Sue's mothering ability was below average, as rated on the mothercraft appraisal score. She had 12 problems, including neglect of medical needs, lack of follow-through on medically prescribed treatment, and insufficient concern to report illness to helping person. Todd's clothing was dirty, he got less than 9 hours of sleep, and he did not have a regular bedtime. Sue was not teaching Todd simple words, and her personal affect was low. For example, she showed little emotion and seemed preoccupied.

Sue described her marital relationship as good during the second interview. John was the decision maker in the family. His business had improved some, and Sue said, "I really should do more to help, but I don't know how." The two boys seemed happy and friendly to the interviewing nurse.

Sue had a checkup before the second interview and then returned to the doctor a month later because her ribs ached and she had a fever, but this was not explained further. She also had an upset stomach and some bad headaches.

Todd was 13 months old now and had not been to a doctor again or received any immunizations. He had been sick with diarrhea, burned his fingers once, and hit his head in a fall. Sue called the doctor after the fall. His sleeping schedule was to go to bed at 10:30 P.M. and wake at 8 A.M. with a 2½-hour nap each day.

Sue's mothering ability was better this time, with four problems noted on the appraisal form. Todd was getting too many sweets and snacks. Sue frequently referred to the opinions of her mother and husband, her speech was still full of pauses, and she did not talk comfortably with the interviewing nurse.

A new public health nurse took over before the third interview, and she brought some new observations to this case. Sue seemed depressed and resigned to her situation—she made only feeble attempts at disciplining Todd, who was very active, opening the door to watch four puppies run in and out of the trailer on a rainy 40° day, and climbing over all the furniture and the nurse. Sue said, "I used to spank him a lot but I just kind of gave up." The interview was interrupted by several phone calls and visits from men who worked for John, and Sue was very noncommital in answering their questions about what to do or what John would want them to do. Sue did exactly what her husband wanted her to do, but this seemed to be more out of fear than respect. She appeared to answer many of the interview questions as she thought they should be answered rather than with her own feelings. The family had no schedule for eating and sleeping, and no adequate health care. The nurse felt that John's dominance was the reason for inadequate care because he would not allow anything that he did not deem necessary.

Sue had been sick with flu, upset stomach, and bad headaches but had not seen a doctor since the second interview.

Todd was now 19 months old. He had been to the doctor once for diarrhea and once to get five stitches after hitting his head in a fall from the table but had not received a checkup or any immunizations. He also had a cold and diaper rash. His diet during the previous 24 hours was adequate in the milk and meat groups with no fruits consumed and only one vegetable portion. Todd's weight and length were above the fiftieth percentile at all three visits, with his weight above the ninety-fifth percentile at 13 months. Thus his weight-for-length was above the ninetieth percentile at both 13 and 19 months.

Sue's mothering ability was very poor now, with 19 problems noted by the nurse on the mothercraft appraisal score. Todd was unwashed, and his clothes were both dirty and inappropriate for the cool weather. He did not have a regular sleeping or eating schedule, and his food intake was not nutritionally adequate. Sue continued to neglect medical needs and did not follow through on prescribed treatment. She spoke in a faint voice, with many pauses and little emotion or warmth. Her conversation was sometimes vague.

The trailer and furniture needed some repairs, and the house was not clean.

As a young mother with a limited education and small income, Sue had few resources to depend on. The family's lack of adequate health care was related to Sue's lack of understanding of the importance of regular care as well as to the family's refusal to accept public assistance. In addition, John did not seem to support Sue, as he apparently saw no need for an increase in health care.

Sue had few contacts outside of her family. Although extended family members lived in the area, she did not emphasize the amount of contact she had with them. It appeared that Sue had very little support from anyone, including her husband, in dealing with her mothering role.

There was no question that Sue loved her children but was having difficulty providing for some of their needs. Todd's lack of immunizations and other health care did not seriously affect his health during the study period but left open the question of his future well-being.

Sylvia and Infant Angela

Sylvia is an 18-year-old Hispanic woman with two small children. At the beginning of this study, her life was upset and unhappy—her husband was very unsupportive, and she left him during the study period. However, several dramatic changes took place, and by the end of the study period Sylvia and her family seemed to be much happier and more stable than before.

Sylvia was born in Texas, one of 13 children. She dropped out of high school and married Richard when she was 16; about the same time she had her first baby, Richard, Jr. She worked in a factory until the sixth month of her second pregnancy, when she moved to a small village in rural Wisconsin with Richard and their son. Two of Richard's brothers lived with them, not paying anything toward household expenses, in a sparsely furnished house. Sylvia was depressed during the pregnancy because Richard was "running around" with another woman, leaving Sylvia feeling trapped and tied down. She hoped to go back to work after the birth and to get a babysitter for the children.

Angela was born shortly after Sylvia's eighteenth birthday, when Richard, Jr., was 13 months old. Sylvia and Richard were then referred to the public health nurse because Sylvia had a gonorrhea infection, which was detected at delivery, and both of them were treated. Apparently this was not the first time that Richard had been treated for venereal disease. Although Sylvia said she had not wanted another child, she had started prenatal care early in the first trimester and continued through to a postpartum exam. She had problems with fainting several times during the pregnancy, which may have been related to heart trouble that she had as a child but which was never fully diagnosed. Angela stayed in the hospital longer than Sylvia because of failure to gain weight; she weighed 5 pounds 15 ounces at birth and continued to have a low weight throughout the study. Sylvia hemmoraged three weeks postpartum and went back to the hospital for a D&C (dilatation and curettage of the uterus).

Richard's brothers moved out shortly after Angela was born, and the family had some extra money to start furnishing their house. Sylvia and Richard's marital problems continued: He spent most of his free time before and after work in a tavern (he worked the 3-to-11 P.M. shift as a molder in a factory), and arrived home late at night expecting Sylvia to get up and prepare dinner for him and his brothers. Sylvia felt Richard did not care for her, but he did not want her to go out at all. Sylvia confided that she felt like killing herself at times, or running away, sometimes with the children and sometimes without them. She needed to have some free time away from the children but did not go back to work and did not find any other alternatives.

Sylvia was quite close to one of her sisters, who lived in the same area, and sometimes got advice about her children from this sister. Sylvia attended church about once a month, did not belong to any clubs, and went out very rarely. She did see friends and relatives often but, aside from her sister, this contact seemed to be more troublesome than helpful. Her two brothers-in-law were cause of more work and problems for her while providing no support to her marriage.

Richard, who was 24 when the study began, had only an elementary school education, and the family income was low although above the poverty level at the time of the first interview. They did not receive any public assistance, but when his brothers moved out of the home, Sylvia and Richard were better able to make ends meet. Most of their marital problems seemed rooted not in financial problems but in the lack of emotional support from Richard, leaving Sylvia totally responsible for the two children. She was able to give the children good physical care, and kept a neat home, but her unhappiness with the marriage impeded a full mothering relationship.

When the first interview took place, Angela was 5 months old. She had not received any well-baby checkups but had seen a doctor several times and had been hospitalized for pneumonia. She had also been sick with diarrhea and a cold and cough, and received the first round of polio and DPT immunizations during one of the visits to the doctor. She was going to bed at 11 P.M. and waking at 8 A.M.

Sylvia's health knowledge and ability to identify home safety hazards were both poor. She reported that she had received very little health care as a child, most of it from emergency-room doctors, although she had frequently been sick. As a young adult, Sylvia obtained some medical care for herself and had been taking the pill for birth control but stopped before her last pregnancy. She started on the pill again after the birth of Angela, saying she definitely did not want any more children. Between Angela's birth and the first interview, Sylvia saw a doctor several times, obtaining a full checkup at one visit as well as being admitted to the hospital for the D&C. She also had problems with feeling tired, insomnia, nerves, upset stomach, flu, and a cold.

The public health nurse found 11 problems when evaluating Sylvia's mothering abilities. Sylvia did not hold Angela very often, except when necessary, and did not verbally interact or play with her. Angela was not getting enough sleep at night. Sylvia seemed to cling to her children and had an air of sadness, displaying little warmth or emotion while talking with the interviewer.

Sylvia reported that she and Richard were divorced between the first and second interviews, and Sylvia moved to California with the children for several months. She returned to Wisconsin before the second interview, when she was living in her brother-in-law's house and taking care of his four children (and her own two) while he was in the hospital. She was planning to move into her own apartment, which she had already selected, as soon as the brother-in-law came home. Although upset about the divorce, Sylvia seemed to be in better health and looked more rested than before. She was trying to make a new life for herself and the children, and she seemed to enjoy her children more, cuddling and playing with them. Sylvia's income was now at poverty level; she received ADC and medicaid assistance, but it was not clear whether or not she received support from Richard. She was not working or planning to work. Sylvia continued to be close to her sister and had in fact lived with her for a while after returning to California. This remained her primary source of social contact as she did not go to church or get out very often.

Sylvia had a number of health problems between the first and second interviews and saw a doctor for breakthrough bleeding associated with taking birth control pills. She also had a cold, flu, upset stomach, bad headaches, nerves, and insomnia but had not contacted a doctor about any of these problems.

Angela was now 13 months old and continued to have some serious health problems. She was hospitalized again, this time for bronchitis, and she saw a doctor when she had a cold, but she had not received any more immunizations and only two checkups, one related to the bronchitis. She also had diarrhea, diaper rash, a cough, and cut her finger on a razor blade, but none of these were serious enough to need medical attention.

Sylvia's mothering had improved quite a bit over the first interview, as rated by the public health nurse. Two of the problems were related to crowding, but the interview took place while the family was sharing space with the brother-in-law's children. Sylvia still did not provide verbal stimulation to Angela, but none of the depression and lack of warmth present before were in evidence now.

Several important changes took place before the third interview. Richard's behavior changed from drinking and running around to attending church and settling down; he said he had been saved, converted to the Assembly of God, and was now a different person. Sylvia revealed that she and Richard had never actually been married, but now that Richard had "been saved," they were formally married after living together again. Until almost the end of the study, Sylvia and Richard had never lived alone—they always had some members of Richard's family with them. Before the third interview, his father, brother, and the brother's girlfriend were living in Sylvia and Richard's home, again not paying anything toward their living expenses. This meant that seven people were living on about $79 per week.

The public health nurse urged Sylvia and Richard to insist on a weekly payment for room and board, which they did, and the three people promptly moved out. Although they later asked to return, they were refused because Sylvia and Richard had come to feel it was wrong to live together out of wedlock. The financial burden caused by the relatives had meant that the family scrimped on food; everyone, including the children, had been eating a lot of starchy foods and few fruits and vegetables.

Richard was working full time in a factory, but the family income fell below poverty level for the first time during the study. They started receiving medicaid and food stamps shortly before the third interview, and their utility bills were paid up for them. Sylvia's sister seemed to be out of the picture at this point, but Sylvia was now actively involved in their new church group. She did not have any other means for social contact as she did not work, belong to clubs, go out, or see relatives. Probably the end of Richard's relatives' dependency was a great boost to Sylvia, although she did not express this openly, but overall it still appeared that she was in need of some social life outside of her family. The family had moved three times since the second interview, ending up in the small village where Angela was born.

Sylvia's health history had continued to be a complex one. Several months before the third interview, she had an abortion which she and Richard had agreed upon because they did not want to have another child out of wedlock. Although she had not wanted another child and was using birth control at least some of the time, Sylvia got pregnant again shortly after she and Richard were married. She had a pain in her side, and her doctor said it was an ectopic pregnancy. He made arrangements for another abortion, but Sylvia did not follow through on this and later felt better, with just some morning sickness. Sylvia was anemic and needed some instruction on good nutrition for herself as well as the children. She also had problems with her tonsils, feeling weakness, a cold, flu, bad headaches, nerves, and insomnia at various times between the second and third interviews. She saw a doctor several times for some of these problems as well as during her pregnancies, and rated her own health as poor.

Angela was 20 months old when the third interview took place. She had been hospitalized several more times for pneumonia, which seemed partially related to the family's poor nutritional intake, but by the time of the interview, it seemed that she had finally recovered completely. She had also been to a doctor for another checkup, and for a cold, diarrhea, and a cough, but she had not been further immunized. Angela's food intake during the 24 hours prior to the interview was adequate for meats and breads but included no fruits and only one serving of milk. Angela's weight was below the twenty-fifth percentile throughout the study while her length jumped over the ninety-fifth percentile at 13 months, falling to below the seventy-fifth percentile at 20 months. Her weight for length was consistently below the fifth percentile. Sylvia rated Angela's overall health as poor while the public health nurse rated it fair, citing the prolonged pneumonia, lack of immunizations, and poor nutrition.

Sylvia's mothering was rated at about the same level as the second interview, but the problems were different. Angela was not fed meals with adequate nutrition and she was not getting enough sleep each night. However, Sylvia's increased enjoyment of her children and the support she got from Richard, as well as his improved interaction with the children, all pointed to the happier environment that had developed.

Sylvia is a young undereducated mother, inadequately prepared to cope with all the demands of two small children. Her health knowledge is limited, and her family's health problems are complicated by the financial strains caused by live-in relatives. The family scrimps on food and had no medical insurance until the end of the study. Sylvia's continuous problems with headaches, weakness, insomnia, and nerves seem evidence of both the pressures of her unstable marriage and the demands of her in-laws. Angela's recurring pneumonia may be linked to her poor nutritional intake and to Sylvia's lack of knowledge about preventive health measures.

Sylvia's social integration was limited throughout this study. Initially her main contacts were family members: a supportive relationship with her sister and a detrimental one with her in-laws. Her husband seemed to change quite dramatically from being unsupportive and uncaring to being involved in the family. But in the end Sylvia still did not have many social contacts; her new church was the only source of contact outside of her family.

The emotional climate in Sylvia's home has greatly improved since the beginning of the study, but several areas still seem open to problems. Sylvia stated openly that she had not wanted another child before Angela was born, and repeated it again before her current pregnancy. The improvement in her marital relationships has not been tested by time or by the birth of the third child. Sylvia continues to carry most of the responsibility for child care, and it remains to be seen whether she will find herself again tied down and limited in her activities.

Vicky and Infant Bruce

Vicky is a 35-year-old white woman living with her husband, Tom, and their three sons in a one-room garage in rural Wisconsin. The family is extremely poor, neither parent has a high school education, and Tom is often unemployed. The children lack adequate medical care, and their intellectual growth seems to be hampered by a lack of stimulation in the home.

Vicky grew up on a farm in rural central Wisconsin, the oldest of eight children. Her father deserted the family and her stepfather was very abusive to her, often expecting her to assume full responsibility for her siblings and to do many farm chores. She attended special-education classes in elementary school and never entered high school, later working in a clothes-cleaning factory. Her husband, Tom, also never entered high school. Their first child, Tom, Jr., was born when Vicky was 26, followed by Greg 2½ years later, and then Bruce 5 years after that, when Vicky was 34. She did not start prenatal care until the sixth month although she was bothered by feeling tired due to anemia during the pregnancy, but she did obtain a postpartum examination. Vicky had never used any birth control up to this point but said that she had not wanted another child before Bruce was born. She started taking the pill after his birth and continued to take it throughout the study, saying she did not want any more children.

Vicky and her family lived in a one-room garage, which she and Tom had purchased for $850 dollars shortly after Greg was born. The garage was unfinished inside, had no plumbing or telephone, and was heated by a wood stove. A small partition separated the boy's bunk bed from the rest of the house. Although Tom was not working when the first interview took place, he did not help Vicky with the chores. She split wood for the stove, carried water in large cans from the neighbor's house, and attended to Greg who had recently had a hernia repaired as well as to Bruce, who had a cold at that time. Tom and Vicky had done nothing to improve the garage, living in it throughout the study period. Near the end of the study the Wisconsin Rural Housing Cooperative started work on finding a mobile home for the family to live in on the same property as the garage. Vicky was very excited at the prospect of a home with running water and a bathroom. Vicky loved animals and kept several dogs, rabbits, and sheep plus many cats.

Tom was laid off from his job as a mechanic for over 6 months, through the first interview, and then found work as a grinder in a foundry. But soon after starting this job, he lost a finger in an accident and was out of work again for several weeks. At the time of the third interview, he was working at a cranberry marsh, repairing machinery. Because of the frequent interruptions to their income and Tom's low educational attainment, the family income was consistently well below poverty level. They received food stamps, medicaid for the children, and unemployment compensation when Tom was laid off.

Vicky visited friends and relatives more than once a week, mentioning her grandmother and aunt as two people she would call on for help or advice about Bruce. She rarely went to church or out to eat, drink, or see a movie, did not belong to any clubs, and did not work during the duration of the study. She loved to chat with the interviewing nurse, talking about her childhood and expressing her opinions openly. Vicky said that her own mother never spent any time with her and that her childhood was very unhappy, but she did not want her three sons to feel that way. However, the interviewing nurse never saw any signs of affection between the parents or between parents and children; Vicky very rarely read to the boys or played with them.

Vicky's attitudes toward seeking medical care for the children improved during the time that the public health nurse was involved. At first the children received little medical attention and Vicky resisted getting prenatal care, but later on she would contact the doctor when one of the boys was sick. She continued to neglect preventive care, including immunizations, although she said she knew it was important. She and Tom "doctored" themselves when sick generally, perhaps partly because their medicaid coverage was only for the children.

Bruce was almost 3 months old at the time of the first interview. He had received one checkup since birth, no immunizations, but was scheduled for the first series of immunizations in a week. He had several illnesses in his first months of life—a cold, cough, flu, and diarrhea—but apparently had been to a doctor only once. He did not have a regular eating schedule but did go to bed regularly at 8 P.M. and wake at 5 A.M.

Vicky had not received any dental or medical care—aside from prenatal care—for about 5 years. She had a cold, flu, upset stomach, bad headaches, and trouble with nerves in the 3 months since Bruce was born.

Vicky's mothering was rated quite poorly by the public health nurse, due in large part to the poor housing and lack of space. In addition, Vicky did not show physical affection for Bruce, stroke him, talk to him, play with him, or handle him more than necessary. She displayed little emotion when discussing her family, said she could not get things done, and seemed dejected at times, ignoring her own appearance.

Bruce was 13 months old when Vicky was interviewed for the second time. He had not received another checkup, but had been to a doctor for two doses of the DPT and polio immunizations as well as for care when he was sick with pneumonia, German measles, a cold, cough, ear infection, eye infection, and infection of a toe. Altogether, Bruce had been to a doctor five times, and the only problem that was not seen by a doctor was his diaper rash. He was now sleeping 10 hours each night with a 1- or 2-hour nap during the day.

Vicky had seen a doctor once since the first interview because she thought she was pregnant, but the test was negative. She continued to take birth-control pills. She had been sick with a cold, flu, upset stomach, bad headaches, and trouble with nerves again but had not sought medical care for any of these problems.

Vicky's mothering improved somewhat over the rating given after the first interview. The housing was still a severe problem, but Vicky's demeanor had improved so that she did not appear to be dejected, and she talked to Bruce now. She continued to ignore his needs for physical affection and contact, and he did not have a regular eating schedule.

Bruce was 18 months old at the third interview. He had not received another physical exam, and Vicky now said that he had received only one dose of the DPT and polio immunizations, not the two she had reported earlier. She said she knew the immunizations were important but had been very lax about keeping them up to date. However, Bruce had been to see a doctor four or five times, for a cold, diarrhea, cough, ear infection, and virus. He was hospitalized for three days with the virus after his temperature rose to 105°. His diet during the 24 hours preceding the interview was adequate in milk consumption only but included some foods in each group except for vegetables. Bruce's length had been near the tenth percentile since he was 3 months old, and his weight was similar until 18 months, when it dropped to below the fifth percentile. His weight for length dropped from above the twenty-fifth to the tenth percentile at 18 months.

Vicky had several health problems since the second interview but again had not seen a doctor or a dentist. She had a cold, flu, bad headaches, and problems with nerves and insomnia.

The third rating of Vicky's mothering by the public health nurse was similar to the second one. There were 8 problems related to the crowded, dilapidated housing and poor furnishings. Bruce did not have a regular bedtime or wake-up time, he was not fed meals with adequate nutritional value, and he spent too much time in the playpen. Vicky continued to neglect his need for physical affection, lacked personal warmth, and had a sense of futility about getting her work done.

Vicky and her family are in a difficult situation, living on a small income and having few personal resources to fall back on. Vicky and Tom are poorly educated, Tom is often unemployed, and when he does work, he can make only a minimal wage. The family is crowded into a one-room house with no indoor plumbing. It seems likely that the impoverished living conditions have contributed to the number of illnesses Bruce had as a baby, although certainly the lack of preventive health care also contributed.

The two older boys were referred to the public health bureau by their school because of immature development and lack of medical care. Their problems are likely to be repeated in Bruce, as his immunizations and checkups are very inadequate, and Vicky gives him very little affection or stimulation. This lack of stimulation from his parents, obtained through talking, reading, playing, or cuddling, may become more detrimental as Bruce grows older.

The family situation should improve when they move into more adequate housing. Vicky's work will be simplified by indoor plumbing and conventional heating, and the additional space may help promote improvements in the family relationships. But the poverty and neglect of preventive medical care will probably continue to be major problems for this family.

Violet and Infant Barbara

Violet is a young white woman with three children under the age of six. Her story is one of a deteriorating marriage, an unemployed husband, and a fairly isolated existence. Barbara, the study infant, lacks adequate medical care, and the emotional needs of all of the children are not being met.

A native of Milwaukee, Violet left school after finishing the ninth grade. Her first child, George, Jr., was born when she was 16, followed by a second child a year later who died at the age of 1 month. Kathy was born when Violet was 18. Violet began using the pill after Kathy's birth, but stopped before becoming pregnant with Barbara. Violet and George were separated for a year before Barbara was born. Violet said that she had not wanted another child at that time and tried to obtain an abortion, but it was denied because she was into the second trimester of pregnancy. She started prenatal care in the fourth month and received a checkup after the birth of Barbara. Violet had worked as a hotel maid, stopping during her pregnancy with Barbara. George had finished the tenth grade in school and was looking for work as a welder or auto mechanic when the study began. Violet was 22, George 23, George, Jr., 5, and Kathy, 3, at this point. Barbara was 2½ months old at the time of the first interview.

The family was living with Violet's parents and two of her teenage siblings, apparently because George was not working. Their annual income for the previous year was below poverty level, and they were receiving AFDC and medicaid assistance. The family income stayed below poverty level through the second interview, when they were receiving food stamps, medicaid, and unemployment compensation. Before the third interview, George started work as a mechanic, they stopped receiving public aid, and their income rose above the poverty level.

Violet said she never went to church, did not belong to any clubs, and went out to eat, drink, or see a movie two or three times a month. She got together with relatives or friends once a week or more throughout the study period. Violet worked a few hours a month, selling women's clothes in her home.

Violet seemed immature to the interviewing nurse and was not getting along well with her husband. She overlooked the emotional needs of the two older children in favor of Barbara, which precipitated a lot of sibling jealousy. Kathy pushed Barbara off a chair and also pushed her off a bed, neither of which resulted in any serious injuries.

Barbara had received a checkup and DPT and polio immunizations before the first interview took place. She had been sick with a cold, cough, throat infection, and a rash. She was on regular eating and sleeping schedules, getting about 11 hours of sleep each night.

Violet had many illnesses and problems since Barbara's birth: cold, flu, upset stomach, headaches, insomnia, nerves, and a rash related to nerves. She said the nerves were due to family problems, and she had tranquilizers to take when needed. She had started taking the pill again, saying that she probably would not have any more children. Her last asymptomatic checkup, excluding prenatal care, had been more than six years ago.

Violet seemed to give good care to Barbara, trying hard to be a good mother. Only six problems in mothering were noted on the mothercraft appraisal form, which is slightly more than average. Violet used an infant seat constantly, did not verbally stimulate Barbara, and lacked warmth in her conversation including times when she was talking about her children.

The family moved twice before the second interview, when they were living with Violet's older sister and her four children, aged 7 to 13. Violet seemed dependent on the interviewing nurse, asking for advice and talking about her current situation. She continued to have marital problems; George was generally unsupportive; they often fought; she felt indecisive and would get too depressed to do much for herself or the children.

Barbara was now a year old. Her foot was burned when she was 6 months old, and when she went to the emergency room for treatment, she also received a checkup. She also had been to an emergency room with a cough and had received another dose of DPT and polio immunizations at some point. She did not see a doctor when she was sick with diarrhea or when she had an allergic reaction to strawberries. She slept 12 hours a night and took a 2- or 3-hour nap each day.

Violet had seen a doctor when she had a sore throat and had also been bothered by an upset stomach and nerves. She continued taking the pill, now saying that she definitely did not want any more children. Violet did not elaborate on her marital problems but did say that her worrying affected her physical well-being.

Violet's mothering ability had seriously deteriorated, as rated by the public health nurse on the appraisal form. She neglected most of the family's medical needs and did not follow through on treatment after getting medical care. Violet rarely talked or crooned to Barbara, giving her very little verbal stimulation or physical affection. Violet was much more dependent on the interviewing nurse in addition to showing signs of apathy and depression. Her conversation was full of pauses and brief answers and she still did not show warmth in discussing her children.

During the time between the second and the third interviews, the family moved to their own apartment. Barbara, now 19 months old, had received one well-baby checkup, not enough to meet a minimum standard. Violet reported that Barbara had received DPT and polio immunizations, but the series was still incomplete. The nurse rated Barbara's health as fair, noting an unevaluated heart murmur and lack of physical exams. Barbara had had colds and a cough and had been to an emergency room twice with diarrhea. She had a lot of minor falls. Her diet as reported in the 24-hour recall was adequate for milk and meat consumption but did not include any green vegetables or fruit. Both her weight and length rose dramatically, to above the ninety-fifth percentile for her age, although her weight for length was below the ninetieth percentile.

The family was at a crisis point when the third interview took place because George had deserted them the night before the nurse visited. Barbara appeared very anxious and afraid of the nurse, the home was disorganized, and Violet was distraught. The nurse noted that the marriage had been unsteady from the start, and both Violet and George were immature. He often hit her. Although he had been employed and the family was not receiving public assistance, Violet was left with over $2000 in bills that she could not pay, including $2000 owed to the county hospital that apparently had been accumulating for some time. She planned to apply for assistance. Violet said that they would not have had "all this bad luck" if George had not broken the mirror seven years ago and seemed to partly believe that was true.

Violet continued to have upset stomachs, bad headaches, trouble with nerves, and rated her own appetite as poor. She had stopped taking the pill but did not say when and reverted to her first interview response to the question about having more children: probably not.

Violet's rating on the mothercraft appraisal form was very similar to the second one, with the same major problem areas.

Violet seemed trapped in a difficult situation as a young, somewhat dependent woman with three small children. She received little emotional support from her husband and had constant difficulties with their relationship. Although she saw her relatives quite often, this did not seem to provide the basis for improving her ability to cope with her personal difficulties. She became more apathetic and depressed as the study contined. Violet had continual physical problems related to her emotional state, including upset stomachs, headaches, and nerves.

Although the family had medicaid coverage, their medical care was poor. Barbara did not receive enough checkups and her immunizations were not regular. Violet and George owed a lot of money for medical care by the third interview, but it is not clear when these bills started piling up. And Violet did not get care for her own medical and emotional problems. After the third interview, with Violet as the sole adult in the household, the importance of her own health becomes crucial. With the end of the daily emotional stresses created by her marriage, perhaps Violet will be able to provide more warmth and care to her children.

6

Sociodemographic Characteristics of Mothers and the Relationship to Mothercraft and Infant Health

The mothers chosen for this study, as described in chapter 3, were likely to be poor but varied in level of income, educational level, age, and race. This chapter will explore the relationship of the sociodemographic characteristics of mothers to their ability in mothercraft, as measured by the Mothercraft Appraisal Score (MAS), attitudes toward using the medical system, and degree of health knowledge.

Research on preventive medical utilization indicates that there is a direct relationship with socioeconomic status (Slesinger 1976; Green 1970). That is, the better the income or education of the person, the more likely he or she is to obtain preventive care. There also is some evidence in national studies that frequency of bed illness and days lost from work is related to income (National Center for Health Statistics 1978). The data reported here, however, are measures of the health of the infant as reported by the mother, which are then related to her sociodemographic characteristics and medical behavior. It will be interesting to see if the usual findings apply.

Two statistical methods of analysis will be employed: Pearsonian correlation coefficients and Multiple Classification Analysis (MCA). The former will be employed to examine zero-order correlations among variables, assuming a linear relationship. MCA is a dummy-variable regression technique that is appropriate when the dependent variable is an interval scale, and the independent variables may be nominal or ordinal ones. This latter technique allows us to examine the relationship of categorical variables to the dependent variable and does not assume that the relationship is linear. In addition, it is possible to calculate the gross and net effects on the dependent variable, when the model is run without (gross) and with controls (net). Further reference to this technique can be found in Andrews et al. 1973. This method also produces statistics equivalent to zero-order correlations (etas) and statistics equivalent to multiple correlations (betas) for each model.

Sociodemographic Characteristics and Mothercraft Appraisal Score

Table 6-1 displays the relationship of each category of the sociodemographic variables to the MAS. Socioeconomic variables are represented by mother's education and poverty status. Income as a separate variable was excluded from the remainder of this analysis because of the redundancy with poverty status, and some evidence of unreliability when some mothers reported family income that included the earnings of her parents or parents-in-law, and some did not. Results in table 6-1 are shown as deviations from the mean score for MAS for the total group, which is − 6.20.

Table 6-1
Multiple Classification Analysis between Sociodemographic Characteristics and Mothercraft Appraisal Score
(Grand mean = − 6.20)

Socioeconomic Characteristics	N	Deviations from Grand Mean	Demographic Characteristics	N	Deviations from Grand Mean
Education			*Race*		
0 – 8	11	− 2.71 ⌐*	Nonwhite	59	− 0.52
9 – 11	65	− 1.89 ⌐ *	White	64	0.48
High school graduate	35	3.20	eta		0.070
College	12	3.45			
eta		0.364***	*Age*		
			14–19	40	− 0.20
Poverty Status			20–24	49	− 0.38
			25–29	18	1.47
Less than 75%	30	− 1.54 ⌐*	30–46	16	0.01
75–99%	43	0.22	eta		0.088
100–124%	13	− 0.88			
125% or more	34	2.55	*Rural/Urban*		
No information	3	—			
eta		0.360**	Rural farm	9	2.31
			Rural nonfarm	18	0.47
			Small urban	13	1.96
			Milwaukee	83	− 0.66
			eta		0.150

***$p \leq$ .001
** $p \leq$ .01
* $p \leq$ .05
† $p \leq$ .10

It is clear that there is a strong, inverse relationship between mother's MAS and the two socioeconomic variables: education and poverty level. The lower her educational attainment or the greater the degree of poverty, the more likely she is to have a negative MAS score.

Several of the cases presented here vividly illustrate this relationship. Vicky had never entered high school, and her family income, including times when her husband was working, stayed below the poverty level during the 17 months under study. Her MAS scores were correspondingly poor: − 25, − 16, and − 16. Debby also follows this pattern of low education, low income and poor MAS scores. Debby had only an elementary school education, had little income and inadequate housing. Her MAS scores were − 24, − 26, and − 23.

Table 6–1 also shows that no significant relationships appear with the demographic variables such as race, age, or rural/urban residence.

Sociodemographic Characteristics and Medical Attitudes and Health Knowledge

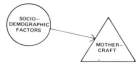

Table 6–2 presents Pearsonian correlation coefficients for the same independent variables shown in table 6–1 with the scores on medical attitudes and health knowledge.

Only a few relationships appear significant among the medical attitudes. Skepticism appears to increase with age and with rurality. Tendency to take the baby to see a doctor for various symptoms appears to be greater among nonwhites, younger mothers, and those in urban areas.

With the health-knowledge items, there is a strong relationship with both education and poverty status. Mothers who have had more education as well as mothers who are not in poverty can identify more safety hazards in the home and have more accurate health information. Demographic characteristics also are related to health knowledge. White women have higher scores than nonwhite women; older mothers have more accurate information about health conditions, although there is no relationship between age and the safety scores; and finally there is a weak positive relationship between health knowledge and rurality.

Ellen typifies a mother with high safety and health-information scores. She identified 12 hazards in the safety picture, and scored 8 out of a possible 10 points on the health-information questions. She completed high school, and with her husband, earned $12,000 to $15,000 per year over the period of the study, a level that was considerably above poverty level for her family. Ellen is white, 31 years old, and lives in Milwaukee.

Table 6–2

Pearsonian Correlation Coefficients between Sociodemographic Characteristics and Measures of Medical Attitudes and Health Knowledge

| Socio-demographic Characteristics | *Medical Attitudes* | | | | *Health Knowledge* | |
| | | | *Propensity to Seek Care* | | | |
	Skepticism	*Prevention*	*For Self*	*For Baby*	*Safety*	*Information*
Socioeconomic						
Education	0.016	0.047	0.154†	− 0.092	0.269**	0.299***
Poverty	0.125	0.098	0.056	− 0.092	0.183*	0.301***
Demographic						
Nonwhite/white	0.116	− 0.000	− 0.009	− 0.252**	0.229*	0.260**
Age	0.201*	− 0.128	0.085	− 0.209*	0.085	0.316***
Rural/urban	− 0.226*	0.011	0.071	0.354***	− 0.169†	− 0.167†

***$p \leq .001$
** $p \leq .01$
* $p \leq .05$
† $p \leq .10$

Sociodemographic Characteristics and Infant Health

Now we turn to the relationship among socioeconomic and demographic variables and the measures of baby's health and illness.

Table 6–3 presents the Multiple Classification Analysis for the six measures of infant health and illness.

First, examining adequacy of baby checkups, we note three variables with statistically significant results. With mother's education, those with some college get significantly more checkups for their babies than mothers with only elementary school education. Also, women who are high school graduates are above the mean in checkup scores, and those who have not finished high school are below the mean. If we look at age, we see it is not the very young women who have poor scores, but rather the older women. Thus we cannot assume it is young women who have not had a chance to finish high school who are the ones not getting checkups for their babies, but rather older women who had not graduated from high school. This is especially true of the mothers 30 and over. And finally, with rural-urban status we see that rural mothers have considerably poorer records in checkups for their infants than urban mothers.

Immunizations, on the other hand, appear to be related only to mother's educational attainment and rural-urban status. Again the higher the mother's educational attainment, the better the immunization record of her infant. And mothers living in rural nonfarm areas have the poorest immunization scores for their infants.

For baby illnesses, mother's poor economic status and her age are significantly related. Mothers whose incomes and family size classify them in poverty report more illnesses for their infants than other mothers. Also, older mothers report significantly *fewer* illnesses than younger mothers for their infants.

Nurse's assessment of the infant's health appears to be significantly related to three variables. Lower assessment scores are found when the mother's educational attainment is low, she is living in poverty, and residing in Milwaukee.

Cases abound with mothers living in poverty who have not had a high school education. Vicky is a good example of such a person. She is an older woman who does not take her child for preventive checkups. She is 35 years old, married, with three children. She and her husband never went to high school. They live in a rural area, in a one-room garage. They are very poor, and Tom is in and out of work frequently. The baby only received one full physical checkup in the first 18 months of his life, and that was before he was 3 months old. The immunization record was no better. Although the aggregate statistics show that the infants of older mothers tend to report fewer illness for their baby, this is not true in Vicky's case. There is a record of considerable illness for baby Bruce. He had pneumonia at 4 months, frequent ear infections, German measles at 5 months, and a serious viral infection at 17 months, for which he was hospitalized. The child was doing poorly, and this was reflected in the weight-for-length record, which was consistently under the twenty-fifth percentile, and, at the third interview, was below the fifth percentile. No doubt a major part of the illness record was due to the severe poverty conditions under which the family lived.

Adequacy of diet is positively related to level of education, being white, and living in a rural area. Weight for length at or above the ninetieth percentile is correlated with being black and living in an urban area.

Linda is an example of a black, urban mother whose child is obese at 20 months. We noted that her baby was often dropped off at relatives and friends, and she had little knowledge of what he ate many days. She never finished high school and rated below average on measures of health knowledge.

Table 6-3
Multiple Classification Analysis between Sociodemographic Characteristics and Infant Health Measures

Sociodemographic Characteristics	N	Deviations from Grand Mean					
		Checkup Score	Immunization Score	Illness Score	Nurse's Assessment	Diet Adequacy	Weight for Length
Grand Mean		(2.18)	(2.23)	(8.93)	(2.15)	(1.94)	(0.30)
Socioeconomic							
Education							
0–8	11	−0.36†	−0.32*	0.61	−0.24	−0.12	0.06
9–11	65	−0.12	−0.23**	0.43	−0.15	−0.20*	0.01
High school graduate	35	0.19	0.26	−1.08	0.31	0.29	−0.04
College	12	0.40	0.77	0.23	0.10	0.39	0.03
eta		0.200	0.292*	0.218	0.316**	0.286*	0.070
Poverty							
Less than 75%	30	−0.15	−0.13	1.06**	−0.25*	−0.14	0.03
75–99%	43	−0.09	−0.13	0.32†	0.11	0.03	0.05
100–124%	13	−0.02	0.23	−0.70	0.16	0.44	−0.15
125% or more	34	0.23	0.24	−1.05	0.09	−0.03	−0.04
No information	3	—	—	—	—	—	—
eta		0.143	0.174	0.262†	0.298*	0.217	0.133

Demographic

Race							
Nonwhite	59	0.04	−0.02	−0.34	−0.06	−0.25 **	0.07 †
White	64	−0.04	0.02	0.32	0.06	0.23	−0.07
eta		0.037	0.020	0.105	0.088	0.275**	0.151†
Age							
14–19	40	0.20 *	−0.10	0.04 †	0.08	−0.04	−0.05
20–24	49	0.09 *	0.04	0.37 *	−0.13	−0.02	0.01
25–29	18	−0.12	0.22	0.29	0.13	−0.05	0.09
30–46	16	−0.62	−0.10	−1.56 †	0.04	0.24	0.01
eta		0.243†	0.096	0.198	0.157	0.110	0.098
Rural/Urban							
Rural farm	9	−0.18	0.11	−1.27	0.41 *	0.50 *	−0.30 *
Rural nonfarm	18	−0.57 *	−0.67 *	0.56	0.30 **	0.33 *	−0.02
Small urban	13	0.13	0.39	−0.17	0.32 *	0.29 †	0.01
Milwaukee	83	0.12	0.07	0.04	−0.16	−0.17	0.04
eta		0.232†	0.255*	0.131	0.342**	0.290*	0.190

*** $p \leq .001$
** $p \leq .01$
* $p \leq .05$
† $p \leq .10$

**Relationship between Mothercraft and Infant Health,
Controlling for Effects of Sociodemographic
Characteristics**

We now return to our original model to see whether or not the relationships we found between mothercraft and infant health measures are explained by the relationships of sociodemographic characteristics to infant health. Table 6–4 displays both the gross and net deviations from the grand mean on four of the dependent measures of infant health. (Illness record was not included because we found in chapter 5 that this variable was not related to mothercraft measures but strongly reflected poverty status. Weight for length was also omitted because it was also not related to mothercraft measures but only to race and rural/urban residence.) The direct relationship between mothercraft measures and the dependent variables are shown in the column labeled "gross;" and the values controlling for the effect of significant sociodemographic variables are shown in the columns marked "net."

Examining first the MAS, we see that it is clearly related to the measures of infant health in the predicted direction. That is, there is a linear and significant relationship between MAS and adequacy of baby checkups, adequacy of immunization, nurse's health assessment, and adequacy of diet of the child.

With checkups, removing the effect of mother's age, education, and rural/urban residence slightly reduces the range of scores but does not erase the relationship.

The same argument applies for immunization scores, nurse's assessment, and diet. In other words, the MAS score, when controlling for the sociodemographic background characteristics that are significantly related to each measure of infant health, still is strongly related.

Health-information and safety scores, however, do not behave this way. When the effect of education and rural-urban residence are controlled, in almost every case, the relationship between the mothercraft measure and infant health measure disappears. Here we note that educational level of mother plays an instrumental part in the score of health information and safety conditions in the home. These findings bear out similar results by Peters and Hoekelman (1973).

One additional statistic in table 6–4 should be observed. Adding the sociodemographic variables that were shown to be significantly related to the dependent variable in all cases increased the correlation (betas) so that almost all the resultant multiple correlations for the final models were significant at or below the .01 level.

Mothercraft Component Score (MCS)

In order to simplify the method of presentation, one additional step was taken. A Mothercraft Component Score was developed by dividing the score on each of the three measures of mothercraft (MAS, health-information and safety scores) at its mean value. Those scores at or above the mean were given a score of 1; those below the mean, 0. The three values were then summed, giving a range of scores from 0 (all poor scores) to 3 (all better than average scores). The grand mean for MCS was 1.83. Table 6–5 presents the MCA analysis of mothercraft component score with six infant health variables. This table demonstrates a significant and linear relationship between the mothercraft component score and three of the measures of infant health, baby checkups, immunization score, and nurse's assessment. The relationship with illness score and diet adequacy is linear, in the predicted direction but not statistically significant.

This table can be compared with the MAS separately, shown previously in table 6–4. We note that the correlation for the component score is lower for checkups and the nurse's assessment, but higher for immunizations. This probably reflects the effect of a good health-knowledge score on the preventive immunization area of baby care. Health knowledge apparently contributes little to the other measures of infant health that is not picked up by the MAS alone.

Table 6–6 shows that all sociodemographic variables (education, poverty status, race, age, and rural-urban residence) are also related to the mothercraft component score. This is in contrast to just the MAS score, which is only related to education and poverty (see table 6–1).

Sandra illustrates a mother who had the poorest score of 0 on the mothercraft component score. Sandra's daughter, Michelle, had no checkups or immunizations during the first 20 months of her life, and the nurse assessed her health at the last interview as fair. Sandra's sociodemographic characteristics also describe the statistical relationship with MCS shown in table 6–6. She did not complete high school, had below poverty level of income, was black, and lived in Milwaukee.

Because of the simplicity of using the three-part mothercraft component score and because it reflects the total score of the MAS, in the final chapter it will occasionally be used in place of the MAS score for data reduction in more complex models.

Table 6–4
Multiple Classification Analysis between Mothercraft Measures and Infant Health Measures, Controlling for Sociodemographic Factors

Mothercraft Measures	N	Deviations from Grand Mean							
		Checkup Score		Immunization Score		Nurse's Assessment		Diet Adequacy	
		Gross	Net[a]	Gross	Net[b]	Gross	Net[b]	Gross	Net[c]
Grand Mean		(2.18)		(2.23)		(2.15)		(1.94)	
Total MAS									
Excellent (0 to −1)	33	0.22**	0.21*	0.35**	0.24*	0.31***	0.23***	0.30**	0.18†
Good (−2 to −4)	36	0.13	0.06	0.11	0.06	0.16	0.13	0.00	−0.03
Fair (−5 to −9)	28	0.11	0.10	−0.05	0.00	−0.07*	0.02	−0.01	0.08
Poor (−10 to −31)	26	−0.56	−0.46	−0.54	−0.39	−0.53	−0.49	−0.37	−0.27
etas and betas		0.276	0.471**	0.270*	0.424**	0.456***	0.557***	0.264*	0.418*

Health-Information Score

High (9–10)	31	0.05 †	0.15	0.35 †	0.25	0.24 *	0.13	0.12	−0.04
Medium (7–8)	53	0.14	0.06	−0.10	−0.13	−0.07	−0.07	0.00	−0.00
Low (3–6)	39	−0.23	−0.21	−0.15	−0.03	−0.10	−0.00	−0.10	0.02
etas and betas		0.151	0.436*	0.179	0.406**	0.209†	0.431**	0.094	0.379*

Safety Score

High (12–17)	32	0.26 *	0.30 †	0.37 **	0.19	0.23 **	0.08	0.28	0.08
Medium (10–11)	44	0.07	0.00	0.07	0.08	0.01	0.03	−0.14	−0.13
Low (1–9)	47	−0.24	−0.21	−0.31	−0.21	−0.17	−0.09	−0.05	0.06
etas and betas		0.191	0.448***	0.236*	0.407**	0.233*	0.426**	0.195	0.393*

[a] Net of education, age, and rural-urban residence.
[b] Net of education and rural-urban residence.
[c] Net of education, race, and rural-urban residence.
*** $p \leq .001$
** $p \leq .01$
* $p \leq .05$
† $p \leq .10$

Table 6–5
Multiple Classification Analysis between Mothercraft Component Score and Measures of Infant Health

Mothercraft Component Score (MCS)		N	Deviations from Grand Mean					
			Checkup Score	Immunization Score	Illness Score	Nurse's Assessment	Diet Adequacy	Weight for Length
Grand Mean			(2.18)	(2.23)	(8.93)	(2.15)	(1.94)	(0.30)
Excellent	(3)	35	0.34 **	0.34 ***	−0.42	0.25 ****	0.17	0.04
Good	(2)	43	0.01	0.28	0.01	0.06	−0.06	−0.02
Fair	(1)	34	−0.18	−0.52	0.21	−0.18	−0.00	−0.01
Poor	(0)	11	−0.54	−0.59	0.61	−0.51	−0.31	−0.03
eta			0.243†	0.356***	0.099	0.338**	0.155	0.060

***p ≤ .001

** p ≤ .01

* p ≤ .05

† p ≤ .10

Table 6–6
Multiple Classification Analysis between Sociodemographic Characteristics and Mothercraft Component Score
(Grand Mean = 1.83)

Socioeconomic Characteristics	N	Deviations from Grand Mean	Demographic Characteristics	N	Deviations from Grand Mean
Education			*Race*		
0–8	11	−0.47 **	Nonwhite	59	−0.22 *
9–11	65	−0.34 ***	White	64	0.20
High school graduate	35	0.57	eta		0.223*
College	12	0.59			
eta		0.481***	*Age*		
			14–19	40	−0.30 *
Poverty Status			20–24	49	0.07
			25–29	18	0.17
Less than 75%	30	−0.33 ***	30–46	16	0.36
75–99%	43	−0.10 **	eta		0.244†
100–124%	13	0.02 †			
125% or more	34	0.55	*Rural/Urban*		
No information	3	—			
eta		0.434***	Rural farm	9	0.62 *
			Rural nonfarm	18	0.00
			Small urban	13	0.32
			Milwaukee	83	−0.12
			eta		0.233†

***$p \leq .001$
** $p \leq .01$
* $p \leq .05$
† $p \leq .10$

7 Sociocultural Setting and Its Relationship to Mothercraft and Infant Health

The purpose of this chapter is to explore the effects of the mother's social situation on her abilities in mothercraft. By social situation or social setting, we mean the degree to which she is socially integrated into both primary and secondary groups; primary referring to family relationships, and secondary referring to attachments and activities in the community.

We hypothesize that mothers who feel themselves a part of a family and who derive social support from its members are likely to be higher on mothercraft skills and also care for the baby in a more adequate way. The converse of this hypothesis is that mothers who feel alone and isolated are less likely to rate well on mothering skills and satisfactory care of the baby. Here we are talking about *primary* ties: relationships with close family relatives and friends.

A *secondary* set of social relationships that binds the individual to the larger community and its institutions also exists. Here we are talking about links to more formal organizations and institutions such as educational institutions, employers, membership in clubs and other groups, as well as church membership and attendance.

Thus we have described two different kinds of support systems: those of a primary nature, centering around the family, and those of a secondary nature, involving the community.

Previous research has indicated that there tends to be a relationship between social integration and utilization of some medical services. Becker and Green (1975) review a number of studies that indicate social integration is clearly related to compliance with medical regimes. For example, the regime of exercise prescribed to patients with coronary heart disease was much more likely to be followed if the patients' wives had positive attitudes toward the regime (Heinzelmann and Bagley 1970). Donabedian and Rosenfeld (1964) studied a group of chronically ill disabled who were discharged from the hospital. Examining the regimes prescribed for each patient, such as diet, medications, and exercise, and the resulting record of compliance after 2 or 3 months, he noted that about 50 percent of the group did not comply with one or more of the recommendations made to them upon leaving the hospital. Only two variables appeared to distinguish among this group: "patients who have help available to them in the home," that is, patients who presumably have social support in the home, and those with more severe disabilities (who were more likely to be in nursing homes). Pilisuk and Froland (1978) review a number of studies on the relationship between illness and social-support networks and, in general, conclude that evidence clearly exists as to the positive contribution a good social-support network makes on individual functioning and health behavior.

Evidence that feelings of social isolation affect help-seeking behavior has also started to accumulate. Bullough (1972) and Morris, Hatch, and Chipman (1966) noted that mothers who expressed feelings of social isolation were less likely to obtain immunization for their infants or postpartum checkups for themselves. They were also less likely to seek family-planning information.

Also in previous research on urban black mothers, the author found that mothers who lived alone with their child or children tended to use fewer preventive medical services than mothers who lived with their husbands. In addition, those single-parent families who lived with extended kin used more services than those living alone, while husband-wife unions living with extended kin used somewhat more than the former but less than the middle-class pattern of husband-wife living alone with their children in one household (Slesinger 1976).

A study on social support and child neglect (Giovannoni and Billingsley 1970) indicated that social contacts with relatives and frequency of church attendance were both related to adequacy of mothering. Also one-parent homes were overrepresented in the neglectful group, while two-parent homes were overrepresented in the adequate parenting group.

Measures of Social Integration

The main independent variable in this analysis is social integration, which has been operationalized into two groups, primary and secondary integration, as mentioned previously. Information from six items in the interview schedule offered information about the level of the mother's integration.

Primary Support System

1. If you need help or advice about your baby, are there people around to help? If yes, who is that?
2. Household composition: Who lives in the household with mother and baby?
3. How often do you get together informally with relatives or friends?

Secondary Support System

1. About how often do you usually attend religious services?
2. Do you belong to any clubs or organizations?
3. How often do you go out for eating, drinking, or seeing a movie?

One additional variable was included to tap the ties with community institutions—whether the mother had any work experience outside the home. This was included because previous research had indicated that mothers who worked outside the home were more likely to use preventive health care for their children (Slesinger 1976). The rationale behind work experience is that contacts are made with people outside the family, babysitters may be employed, and the mother has experience in dealing with people in a number of impersonal institutions as well as the institution for which she works.

Social Integration and Mothercraft Appraisal Score

Table 7-1 shows the results of the MCA analysis, displaying the deviations from the grand mean of the MAS and the MCS for the various integration measures. Looking first at measures of primary group integration, we note that only one component, household composition, appears consistently and significantly related to the MAS or MCS in the hypothesized direction. That is, mothers with males present in the home have better appraisal scores than those without males in the home. Although not shown in the table, the presence of extended family members does not significantly affect the scores.

Another finding of interest is the response to the question of whether the mother can call on someone for help or advice about the baby. Contrary to our hypothesis, those who reply ''no one'' have significantly better scores than those who give the name or relationship of a person. The women who mention their mothers as assisting are above the MAS mean of the total group but not as high as those who reply ''no one.'' Those who mention other people (for example, sister, husband, babysitter, or a sibling of baby) have scores below the mean of the total group.

Another result that only partially supports the hypothesis is the frequency of visiting friends and relatives. First, those who say they rarely visit friends and relatives are numerically few but have very low MAS scores, whereas those who visit 2–3 times a month have MAS scores above the mean of the total group. However, the relationship is not linear: If they visit with relatives or friends once a week or more, the MAS is below the mean. One can speculate that a number of the unwed mothers who did a great deal of socializing may be in the latter group. This will be discussed further when we examine the demographic characteristics of the mothers.

Among the secondary group integration variables, two, church attendance and work experience, appear to be significantly related to the MAS. The contrast between those who attend church once a week or more compared with all the other groups is also statistically signficant. Mothers who attend church at least once a week have significantly better scores on both indexes. Those who have had some work experience also have significantly higher MAS and MCS scores than those who have never worked. Also supporting our hypothesis, although not statistically significant with MAS, club members had higher scores than those who did not belong to clubs.

Two vignettes illustrate the range of social relationships the mothers have. Cora is in a stable marriage and is an active member of some groups in secondary institutions as well. She has had a long-term commitment to her church and actively involves herself in projects at both her church and the school her older children attend. She also had worked as a Head Start driver before the birth of Cindy and returned to that job by the time of the third interview. Beth, on the other hand, typifies an isolated mother. She is on public assistance and does not work. She has no husband but seems to move in with one boyfriend after another. She almost never attends church and reports a string of different people she can call on to help with her baby at different times. She lived in a different place at each interview and told the nurse she had moved several more times. Her mothercraft appraisal score worsened over time, and at the last interview the nurse was quite concerned what the future might hold for baby Tony.

The variable that taps socializing outside the home, Go out, similar to the case for visiting friends and relatives, does not show a linear relationship with the MAS or MCS. Those who go out only a few times a year to restaurants, movies or bars have the highest scores; those who rarely go out have the lowest. These differences, however, are not statistically significant.

Table 7-1
Multiple Classification Analysis between Social Integration Measures, Mothercraft Appraisal Score, and Mothercraft Component Score

Social Integration Measures	(N)	Deviations from Grand Mean	
		MAS	MCS
Grand Mean		(−6.20)	(1.83)
Primary Integration			
Help with Baby			
No one	11	2.74 †	−0.01
Mother	58	0.68	−0.02
Other	54	−1.29	0.02
eta		0.180	0.021
Household Composition			
No male present	51	−1.88 *	−0.42 ***
Male present	72	1.33	0.30
eta		0.224*	0.373***
Friends/Relatives			
Visit rarely	5	−3.40	−0.43
Few times/year	12	−0.30	0.09
2–3 times/month	33	1.89 †	0.38 **
Once a week or more	73	−0.57	−0.16
eta		0.181	0.265*
Secondary Integration			
Church Attendance			
Never	24	−1.26 **	−0.12 †
Few times/year	39	−0.80 **	−0.29 **
1–3 times/month	31	−1.68 **	0.11
Once a week or more	29	3.92	0.38
eta		0.312**	0.273*
Club membership			
No	98	−0.40	−0.11 **
Yes	25	1.56	0.45
eta		0.111	0.241
Go out			
Rarely	25	−1.92	−0.27
Few times/year	27	2.57	0.21
2–3 times/month	46	−0.26	−0.00
Once a week or more	25	−0.36	0.05
eta		0.212	0.167
Work Experience			
Yes	103	1.14 ***	0.13 ***
No	20	−5.85	−0.68
eta		0.365***	0.317***

***$p \leq .001$

** $p \leq .01$

* $p \leq .05$

† $p \leq .10$

Sociodemographic Characteristics and Social Integration

Let us examine the correlation coefficients between socioeconomic and demographic characteristics and measures of social integration (see table 7-2). First, looking at statistically significant relationships between sociodemographic and primary integration variables, there appear to be two: household composition and visiting with friends and relatives. All sociodemographic variables are statistically significantly related to whether there is a husband or male partner present in the home. Those who are more likely to have a male in the home are more likely to be better educated, not in poverty, white, older, and living in a rural area. Only mother's age is related to visiting patterns, with younger mothers more likely than older women to visit with friends and relatives frequently. This lends some support to the speculation made previously that the younger women may be the ones who socialize a great deal and have poorer MAS scores.

Marcia fits this pattern during the first two waves. She is single, 18 years old, visits friends and relatives once a week or more, and her MAS is below the mean. She is very busy with the demands of a job and going to school, but this may have also brought her into contact with more people that she visited socially as well. She apparently had no boyfriend, which may also have led to a desire for more social life.

Examining the secondary social-integration measures, all but one variable, frequency of going out to eat or for entertainment, are significantly related in some way to sociodemographic characteristics of the mothers. One measure of secondary integration is most strongly related to the sociodemographic variables, that is, church attendance. Those who attend church more frequently are likely to be better educated, not in poverty, white, older, and living in a rural area. Club membership is also significantly related to higher education, being white and living in a rural area. Work experience is related to higher educational attainment and not living in poverty.

To recapitulate, we have seen that both primary and secondary social-integration measures are related to the mothercraft appraisal scores. Women who are more socially integrated have better mothercraft scores. We have also seen that socioeconomic and demographic characteristics are related to social-integration measures, particularly to the measures of household composition, church attendance, club membership, and previous work experience.

Table 7-2
Pearsonian Correlation Coefficients between Sociodemographic Characteristics and Measures of Social Integration

Sociodemographic Characteristics	Primary Integration			Secondary Integration			
	Help with Baby	Household Composition	Visits with Friends/ Relatives	Church Attendance	Clubs	Go Out	Work Experience
Socioeconomic							
Education	0.019	0.159†	0.010	0.196*	0.254**	0.024	0.271**
Poverty	0.143	0.298***	0.089	0.304***	0.150	0.090	0.367***
Demographic							
Nonwhite/white	0.041	0.447***	0.029	0.170†	0.242**	0.048	0.073
Age	0.062	0.287***	−0.203*	0.212*	0.076	−0.141	0.075
Rural/urban	−0.081	−0.394***	−0.015	−0.364***	−0.196*	−0.025	−0.041

*** $p \le .001$

** $p \le .01$

* $p \le .05$

† $p \le .10$

Relationship between Integration and Mothercraft, Controlling for Sociodemographic Effects

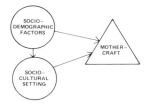

We are now to address the question:

> Will mothers who are more socially integrated have higher appraisal scores than those who are less integrated, controlling for socioeconomic status or demographic background statistics?

Table 7-3 is based on the gross models presented in table 7-1, eliminating the two integration measures, help with the baby and going out socializing, which were not significantly related. In addition, table 7-3 presents net models that control for the effect of socioeconomic variables that had been found to be related to the integration measures at .05 level of significance or better.

The answer to the preceding question, from analysis of data in table 7-3 is a qualified yes; mothers who are more socially integrated will have higher mothercraft scores, even when taking into account the sociodemographic factors that are related to the integration variables. In other words, for example, mothers who have no male present in the household have poorer MAS and MCS scores than those who have a male present. From previous analyses, we know that the households without males present are more likely to be poor, black, young, and urban. Controlling statistically for all these characteristics, mothers without a male present are still likely to have lower mothercraft scores than those who have males in the household.

In constructing table 7-3, three separate models were run: (1) only socioeconomic variables were added as a control, (2) only demographic controls were added as a control, and (3) both sets of variables were added in one model. Only the final model is presented in table 7-3. However, for all the social-integration variables, adding education and/or poverty as a control consistently reduces the differential between categories. Adding the demographic variables of age, race, and/or rural-urban residence did not reduce the differential substantially.

Thus we can conclude that although socioeconomic status strongly influences the likelihood of the mother's social integration both on a primary and secondary level, when we control for these factors, mother's social-integration patterns are still related to the quality of mothering. The strongest relationships remain with household composition, church attendance, and work experience.

Table 7-3
Multiple Classification Analysis between Social Integration Measures and Mothercraft Scores, Controlling for Sociodemographic Factors

Social Integration Measures	*N*	*Deviations from Grand Mean* — *Mothercraft Appraisal Score*		*Mothercraft Component Score*	
Grand Mean		(−6.20)		(1.83)	
		Gross	*Net*	*Gross*	*Net*
Primary Integration					
Household Composition[a]					
No male present	51	−1.88 *	−1.62 †	−0.42 ***	−0.25 *
Male present	72	1.33	1.14	0.30	0.18
eta and beta		0.224*	0.424*	0.373***	0.534***
Friends/Relatives[b]					
Visit rarely	5	−3.40	−3.42	−0.43	−0.48
Few times/year	12	−0.30	−0.18	0.09	0.06
2–3 times/month	33	1.89 †	1.85	0.38 **	0.30 *
Once a week or more	73	−0.57	−0.57	−0.16	−0.11
eta and beta		0.181	0.195	0.265*	0.322*
Secondary Integration					
Church Attendance[c]					
Never	24	−1.26 **	−0.94 †	−0.12 †	0.02
Few times/year	39	−0.80 **	−0.16 †	−0.29 **	−0.12
1−3 times/month	31	−1.68 **	−1.78 *	0.11	0.09
Once a week or more	29	3.92	2.90	0.38	0.05
eta and beta		0.312**	0.540**	0.273*	0.596***
Club Membership[d]					
No	98	−0.40	−0.12	−0.11 **	−0.05
Yes	25	1.56	0.46	0.45	0.21
eta and beta		0.111	0.378*	0.241**	0.514***
Work Experience[e]					
Yes	103	1.14 ***	0.66 *	0.13 ***	0.05
No	20	−5.85	−3.38	−0.68	−0.27
eta and beta		0.365***	0.502	0.317***	0.571***

[a]Net model includes: poverty, age, race, rural-urban residence.
[b]Net of age.
[c]Net of education, poverty, age, rural-urban residence.
[d]Net of education, race, rural-urban residence.
[e]Net of education, poverty.
***$p \leq .001$
** $p \leq .01$
* $p \leq .05$
† $p \leq .10$

The statements made above pertain to both the mothercraft appraisal score and to the mothercraft component score, which adds health-knowledge items to the MAS. However, because health knowledge was strongly related to education, it can be seen in table 7-3 that when educational level is controlled in a model for the MCS, significant differences between categories disappear. The multiple correlation coefficient, however, increases substantially.

Marcia and Jerry illustrate both the importance of some social-support members in the household if the father of the baby is not around and the importance of educational attainment. Marcia lives with her mother, four teenage sisters and brothers, and two sons of her 16-year-old sister. She completed high school and had some secretarial training. She quickly went to work after the baby was born, and soon changed jobs to become a counseling aide in a community-service agency. She attended Milwaukee Area Technical College in the mornings, and worked in the afternoon and evenings. So baby Jerry was left with a babysitter during the days and with her family at night.

Although at first the baby was not receiving much love and attention from Marcia, by the time the child was 19 months old, she had relaxed more and was interacting well when she was home with her child.

Marcia knew what medical regimes should be followed with her baby and saw to it that Jerry had his checkups and immunizations. Marcia's mother and family saw to it the child received the love and attention he required. Whereas the MAS was -16 at the first interview, it had dropped to -1 by the third interview when Jerry was 19 months old.

Relationship between Mothercraft and Infant Health Measures, Controlling for the Effects of Significant Integration Variables

Let us now examine what happens to the relationship between mothercraft and infant health when we control on the social-integration experience of the mother.

Three social-integration variables are strongly related to mothercraft scores: household composition, church attendance, and work experience. Table 7-4 shows the relationship of MAS to each infant health measure. The gross relationship is displayed, then three separate models, controlling for one integration measure at a time. The final model includes the effect of all three integration variables as controls.

The conclusion from examining table 7-4 is that integration plays very little part in changing the relationship between mothercraft and infant health, when health is measured by preventive checkups, immunization record, nurse's assessment and adequacy of diet and the health of the child. No pattern, once again, is displayed with number of illnesses the infant experienced or weight for length.

Comparison of the Effects of Sociodemographic versus Social-Integration Variables on the Relationship between Mothercraft and Infant Health

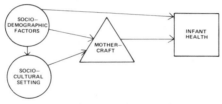

Table 7-5 summarizes some statistics obtained in the analyses performed previously, in order to compare the relative importance of sociodemographic factors and social-integration ones. The table displays multiple correlation coefficients resulting from various MCA models presented previously. We note the following:

1. Looking first at the gross relationship between the mothercraft scores and each infant health measure, in every case except the immunization score, the correlation is higher for mothercraft appraisal score (MAS) than the mothercraft component score (the MAS plus health-knowledge score).

2. For all infant health measures except adequacy of diet, adding the sociodemographic variables explains more variance than the social-integration components.

3. In all infant health measures, rural-urban residence contributes more than educational level to explained variance. The importance of the rural-urban location of the mothers on preventive medical care is investigated in detail in Slesinger (1980a). We do not mean to imply,

Table 7-4
Multiple Classification Analysis between Infant Health Measures and Mothercraft, Controlling on Social-Integration Variables

Mothercraft Appraisal Score (MAS)	N	Gross	Net of Household Composition	Net of Church Attendance	Net of Work Experience	Net of All
		Checkup Score (Grand Mean = 2.18)				
MAS						
Excellent	33	0.22**	0.30**	0.25**	0.24**	0.33**
Good	36	0.13	0.13	0.16	0.15	0.16
Fair	28	0.11	0.06	0.08	0.09	0.03
Poor	26	-0.56	-0.62	-0.63	-0.61	-0.69
eta and beta		0.276*	0.334**	0.311†	0.290*	0.354*
		Immunization Score (Grand Mean = 2.23)				
MAS						
Excellent	33	0.35**	0.37**	0.38**	0.33	0.38**
Good	36	0.11	0.11	0.11	0.09	0.10
Fair	28	-0.05	-0.06	-0.05	-0.04	-0.06
Poor	26	-0.54	-0.55	-0.58	-0.51	-0.56
eta and beta		0.270*	0.275†	0.295†	0.274†	0.300
		Illness Score (Grand Mean = 8.93)				
MAS						
Excellent	33	-0.54†	-0.58†	-0.29	-0.63†	-0.48
Good	36	0.15	0.15	0.31	0.08	0.25
Fair	28	-0.33	-0.30	-0.51	-0.28	-0.42
Poor	26	0.83	0.86	0.31	0.99	0.70
eta and beta		0.162	0.165	0.289	0.186	0.319

Nurse's Assessment (Grand Mean = 2.15)

MAS	N	(1)	(2)	(3)	(4)	(5)
Excellent	33	0.31 ***	0.30 ***	0.31 ***	0.30 ***	0.31
Good	36	0.16 *	0.16 *	0.15 *	0.16 *	0.15
Fair	28	-0.07	-0.07	-0.06	-0.07	-0.07
Poor	26	-0.53	-0.53	-0.52	-0.52	-0.53
eta and beta		0.456***	0.456***	0.483***	0.457***	0.483***

Diet Adequacy (Grand Mean = 1.94)

MAS	N	(1)	(2)	(3)	(4)	(5)
Excellent	33	0.30 **	0.29 **	0.24 *	0.29 **	0.23 *
Good	36	0.00	0.00	-0.02	-0.01	-0.04
Fair	28	-0.01	-0.01	0.01	-0.01	0.02
Poor	26	-0.37	-0.36	-0.29	-0.34	-0.26
eta and beta		0.264*	0.264†	0.307†	0.270†	0.485

Weight for Length (Grand Mean = 9.72)

MAS	N	(1)	(2)	(3)	(4)	(5)
Excellent	33	0.03	0.05	0.04	0.04	0.06
Good	36	-0.05	-0.05	-0.06	-0.05	-0.05
Fair	28	-0.05	-0.06	-0.04	-0.05	-0.05
Poor	26	0.08	0.08	0.08	0.08	0.06
eta and beta		0.122	0.139	0.265	0.126	0.282

Table 7-4 continued.

Mothercraft Component Score (MCS)	N	Gross	Net of Household Composition	Net of Church Attendance	Net of Work Experience	Net of All
			Checkup Score (Grand Mean = 2.18)			
MCS						
Excellent	35	0.34**	0.51****	0.40***†	0.37**	0.57*****
Good	43	0.01	-0.02	-0.01	0.02	-0.02
Fair	34	-0.18	-0.28	-0.20	-0.21	-0.32
Poor	11	-0.54	-0.67	-0.65	-0.60	-0.77*
eta and beta		0.243†	0.348**	0.293	0.258†	0.379*
			Immunization Score (Grand Mean = 2.23)			
MCS						
Excellent	35	0.34***	0.43*****	0.34***	0.34***	0.41***
Good	43	0.28	0.27	0.28	0.28	0.27
Fair	34	-0.52	-0.57	-0.52	-0.52	-0.56
Poor	11	-0.59	-0.65	-0.58	-0.58	-0.62
eta and beta		0.356***	0.372**	0.364*	0.356**	0.378*
			Illness Score (Grand Mean = 8.93)			
MCS						
Excellent	35	-0.42	-0.52	-0.18	-0.53	-0.46
Good	43	0.01	0.03	-0.01	-0.02	-0.04
Fair	34	0.21	0.27	0.15	0.32	0.39
Poor	11	0.61	0.68	0.16	0.77	0.43
eta and beta		0.099	0.109	0.262	0.133	0.300

Nurse's Assessment (Grand Mean = 2.15)

MCS	n					
Excellent	35	0.25 ****	0.26 ***	0.21 ***	0.24 ***	0.22 ***
Good	43	0.06	0.06	0.07	0.06	0.06
Fair	34	-0.18	-0.18	-0.17	-0.16	-0.17
Poor	11	-0.51	-0.51	-0.44	-0.49	-0.44
eta and beta		0.338**	0.338**	0.372**	0.343**	0.376*

Diet Adequacy (Grand Mean = 1.94)

MCS	n					
Excellent	35	0.17	0.15	0.14	0.14	0.12
Good	43	-0.06	-0.06	-0.05	-0.07	-0.07
Fair	34	-0.00	0.01	0.00	0.03	0.03
Poor	11	-0.31	-0.29	-0.25	-0.26	0.11
eta and beta		0.155	0.157	0.262	0.181	0.277

Weight for Length (Grand Mean = 9.72)

MCS	n					
Excellent	35	0.04	0.07	0.03	0.05	0.06
Good	43	-0.02	-0.03	-0.02	-0.02	-0.02
Fair	34	-0.01	-0.02	-0.00	-0.02	-0.03
Poor	11	-0.03	-0.05	-0.00	-0.04	-0.03
eta and beta		0.060	0.107	0.241	0.086	0.266

*** $p \leq .001$
** $p \leq .01$
* $p \leq .05$
† $p \leq .10$

Table 7–5
Comparison of the Effect of Sociodemographic and Social-Integration Factors on Infant Health Measures in Additive Models (Multiple Classification Analysis)
(etas and betas)

Mothercraft Scores	Gross	Mothercraft Score plus Sociodemographic Variables				Mothercraft Score plus Social-Integration Variables[a]

Checkup Score

		Education	*Rural/Urban*	*Age*	*Education, Rural/Urban and Age*	
MAS	0.276	0.306†	0.365**	0.377**	0.471**	0.354*
MCS	0.243†	0.264	0.355*	0.387**	0.477**	0.379*

Immunization Score

		Education	*Rural/Urban*		*Education and Rural/Urban*	
MAS	0.270*	0.344*	0.369**		0.424**	0.300
MCS	0.356***	0.420***	0.434***		0.481***	0.378*

Illness Score

		Poverty		*Age*	*Poverty and Age*	
MAS	0.162	0.296		0.246	0.390*	0.319
MCS	0.099	0.268		0.215	0.375†	0.300

Nurse's Assessment

		Education	*Rural/Urban*		*Education and Rural/Urban*	
MAS	0.456***	0.488***	0.545***		0.557***	0.483***
MCS	0.338**	0.389**	0.452***		0.474***	0.376*

Diet Adequacy

		Education	*Rural/Urban*	*Race*	*Education, Rural/Urban and Race*	
MAS	0.264*	0.337*	0.373**	0.368**	0.418*	0.485
MCS	0.155	0.292	0.316†	0.299*	0.393*	0.277

Table 7–5 continued.

Mothercraft Scores	Gross		Mothercraft Score plus Sociodemographic Variables		Mothercraft Score plus Social-Integration Variables[a]
		Weight for Length			
		Race	*Rural/Urban*	*Race and Rural/Urban*	
MAS	0.122	0.199	0.230	0.250	0.282
MCS	0.060	0.180	0.216	0.243	0.266

[a]Social-Integration variables are household composition, church attendance, and work experience.
*** $p \leq .001$
** $p \leq .01$
* $p \leq .05$
† $p \leq .10$

however, that the social-integration factors are not important. However, for receipt of medical care of a preventive nature, apparently structural factors such as location and level of mother's education play a vital role, whereas other elements play a lesser role.

4. Illness score is a special way of measuring infant health. It clearly responds to poverty level (within this low-income group). Poverty connotes poor nutrition, inadequate housing, and insufficient clothing, all of which may contribute to lowered resistance to germs and disease. A second variable that affects illnesses is the age of the mother. Apparently, babies whose mothers are older tend to have fewer reported illnesses. One caveat must be mentioned. It is possible that older mothers, who may be more experienced, may tend to overlook a period of illness for the child whereas the younger mother may be more conscious of each illness episode.

8 Summary and Discussion

This book describes the effects of mothering—specifically, poor-quality mothering—on the health of infants in a "typical" or "normal" population. Previous research has indicated that in highly atypical cases of extreme maternal deprivation, social isolation, or severe maternal personality disorders, the quality of nurturing is poor and adversely affects the health and development of the child. Little was known, however, about the effects of less extreme deprivation on the development and health of the child. Thus the purpose of this study was to follow a set of "normal" mothers of newborns as their children aged. The mothers chosen for the study had some social and structural characteristics that have been associated with child neglect in previous studies. In this way the author anticipated seeing what happens in the day-to-day lives of these women that determines poor mothering and in turn affects the children's health and development.

For this purpose a prospective and exploratory study was designed. It was prospective so that predictive conditions could be identified near the time of the birth and mothers followed to determine their mothercraft skills as time passed. The research was exploratory because measures of quality of mothering had to be developed, cases of inadequate mothering had to be identified, and ways of following the family over a period of time had to be devised.

The initial task was to evaluate quality of mothering. Mothercraft skills are difficult to measure. We defined mothering ability as having the following components:

Management of the child's *physical environment;* providing adequate housing conditions and material attributes

Provision of adequate levels of *physical care* of the child such as food, clothing, rest, and medical care

Provision of positive and minimal levels of *emotional and cognitive stimulation and interaction* with the child

Absence of aspects of mother's *personality* that may adversely affect her interaction with child such as dependency, apathy, lack of verbal expression or affect, and communication skills

Knowledge of basic child-related health information, including awareness of safety hazards in the home.

A series of specific statements—called the mothercraft appraisal form—was constructed to measure each of the preceding components. This technique was previously used by Polansky and colleagues (1972, 1975) in a study of child neglect in Appalachian homes. In addition, mother's knowledge of infant health care was determined by a series of questions asked of the mother in the interview.

A second task was to find appropriate indexes of infant health. Multiple measures of infant health were collected. They included:

A record of immunizations at 20 months

A record of well-baby checkups for the first 20 months

Number of illnesses reported by mothers over the life of the child

A registered nurse's general assessment of the health of the infant based on a physical assessment and medical history obtained at 20 months

Evaluation of adequacy of diet at 20 months

Weight and length measurements at 3, 12, and 20 months

A few additional measures were also collected but turned out not to be useful. They included the results of the Denver Development Screening Test, administered at three age intervals, and the number of accidents the child experienced as reported by the mother at each interview. The former did not discriminate among the infants; only two children exhibited developmental delays. The latter, the number of reported accidents, appeared to be quite inconsistent from one mother to another. That is, what one mother considered an accident was regarded by another as a minor occurrence, not worth reporting.

Model

The following model was proposed that relates variation in infant health to mothercraft:

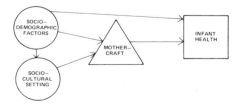

This model suggests two antecedent groups of factors that affect mother-craft: sociodemographic factors such as age, race, education, poverty status, and rural/urban residence; and sociocultural setting, referring essentially to the mother's social environment. Two levels of social support were noted: primary ties the mother has developed with family and friends and is able to utilize for social support and ties with institutions and organizations that may help the mother utilize community resources.

We hypothesized that structural constraints such as mother's very young age, severe poverty, or low educational attainment would have a direct effect on the quality of mothering. In addition, the sociodemographic factors would also affect the sociocultural component—the social environment that surrounds the mother and infant.

Measures used to operationalize primary integration in this study included availability of someone to help with or give advice about the baby; presence of other adults in the household; and frequency of visiting with relatives and friends. Secondary integration was measured by church attendance, club membership, going out for social activities, and working at a job outside the home. We hypothesized that women tied into a strong social-support network would be more likely to be able to counter the adverse effects related to young age, little education, and economic problems. In addition, ties with institutions outside the home were hypothesized to aid in utilizing medical services.

Method and Sample

Because of the exploratory nature of this research and the difficulty of locating poor-quality mothering in a random sample of recent births, case screening was employed for selection of the study mothers. Public health nurses were asked to visit homes of newborns, and identify households in which mothers faced social and structural conditions deemed likely to affect quality of mothering, as indicated by previous research. These conditions included poverty, low educational attainment, large number of children with close spacing intervals, and very young mothers.

Mothercraft appraisal scores were calculated at each interview, based on ratings made by the public health nurses following each home visit. The correlations between the appraisal scores at each interview were .704 between the first and second interview; .662 between the second and third interview; and .501 between the first and third interview. The range of negative items decreased by the time of the third interview. For the first, the scores ranged from 0 to -42; for the second, the scores ranged from 0 to -43; for the third interview, the range was 0 to -31.

Because we wanted to examine mothercraft skills exhibited by the mother when her baby was 20 months, we analyzed only the relationship between the final appraisal evaluation and scores that reflect the cumulative experience of the child.

Research was conducted in a large city and four rural counties in the Midwest. One hundred forty-eight households were identified; of these, 123 mothers and infants were followed over a 17-month period, from the time the babies were about 3 months old to the time they were 20 months old. The first interview was held at 3 months, the second was around the child's first birthday, and the final interview was conducted when the infant was about 18 to 20 months old. This latter time point was chosen because of organizational constraints on the project, not because of specific developmental points in the life of the child. That is, while the public health nursing units cooperating with this project agreed to absorb the time and costs for following a specific set of children (some of whom were not included in their usual case load), they could not do so for more than 2 years. At each of the three home visits, each mother was interviewed and her baby weighed, measured, and examined. After each interview, when the nurse had left the home, she completed the mothercraft appraisal form, which was the major basis of evaluating mothering performance.

The sample mirrors characteristics of families in poverty, residing in both central cities and rural areas. About 70 percent of the urban sample was black, and the entire rural sample was white. About 70 percent of the total group was at or below the poverty level. About 60 percent of the mothers had not completed high school, with a larger proportion (70 percent) in the urban compared to the rural (46 percent) areas. Ages of the mothers ranged from 15 to 45 at time of the birth, and the birth order of the study baby varied from first to eleventh birth. Eighty-seven percent of the rural mothers were married, compared to about 37 percent of the urban mothers.

Findings

Only three of the six measures of infant health were significantly correlated with the mothercraft appraisal: child's checkup record over the 20 months (.274 at a .01 level of significance); the final immunization record (.244 at a .01 level of significance); and nurse's assessment of the general health status of the child at 20 months (.238 at a .01 level of significance). These measures also were correlated with mother's education and rural/urban residence. The better educated the mother, the better the checkup and immunization records. And the children of the urban mothers had better checkup and immunization records than those of rural mothers. In addition, children of younger mothers had better checkup records than children of older mothers.

It should be noted that the strong statistical relationships found with checkups and immunizations reflected the likelihood of using the medical system, not necessarily the health of the infant. Previous research has consistently shown a relationship between education and utilization of medical services (Green 1970; Bullough 1972). The present research not only demonstrates this relationship but also shows an interesting relationship with rural/urban residence. Lack of accessibility hampers rural mothers more than urban mothers in their utilization of preventive medical care for their infants (Slesinger 1980a). This point supports similar findings by Aday and Andersen (1975) who conceptualize a set of "enabling" factors.

Mother's reports of illnesses in these data were related only to poverty status. Illnesses were measured by occurrences of seven conditions: colds, diarrhea, flu, ear infections, diaper rash, other rashes, and other (which included infectious diseases and other less frequent conditions).

Diet adequacy appeared to be related to mother's level of education. In addition, it is interesting to note that rural babies in the sample had better diets than the urban babies. Studies of birth weight of infants have indicated that rural areas produce fewer low-weight births than urban areas, controlling for race (National Center for Health Statistics 1980). Weight-for-length measurements indicated that about one out of three babies were at or above the ninetieth percentile at 12 and 20 months. The obesity finding is puzzling and will be further discussed.

The sociocultural component of our model was more complex than anticipated. For example, it was hypothesized that mothers living alone with their children would be more isolated and least socially integrated. It was anticipated that living with extended family members would provide the mother with some degree of primary integration, but the strongest integration would be found where a male partner was present. In general, this turned out to be true. However, classifying the household composition at three time points in a 17-month period revealed important new information. In the course of following the families, we learned that the amount of change within household composition over a relatively short period of time is sometimes substantial. For example, of the mother-child units who were living alone at the first interview, 43 percent did not remain alone over the 17-month period (Slesinger 1980b). The husband-wife units were the most stable over time, with 83 percent experiencing no change over the 17 months.

In addition, not all social-integration patterns with relatives were positive ones. The male in the household often was an asset; he provided financial and social support and was a full partner in the childrearing activities. Sometimes, however, the male was a distinct disadvantage—both financial and emotional. A case exemplifying a poor husband was that of Violet who had severe marital problems and resulting depression that culminated when her husband deserted the family. Extended families are also often considered a supportive network. Marcia used her family for babysitting plus a great deal of emotional and cognitive interactions with her child. On the other hand, Sylvia had nothing but problems when she had the responsibility of caring for her brother's children on top of her own problems.

Work experience as a measure of ties with the larger community appeared to be an important measurement of secondary integration. Women who work must keep schedules, arrange for child care, be responsible for getting somewhere on time, and accept a commitment to outside institutions and personnel to appear for work despite problems involving others, including her baby, at home. She also must be able to communicate with some degree of success with strangers. All these factors also make it likely that this mother will be able to make a doctor's appointment, show up for the appointment, get there reasonably on time, and be able to communicate with nurses, secretaries, aides, and doctors about the health or illness of her child. Another key element in work experience is the money earned from the work. This element provides income, although, of course, there may be expenses that reduce this income considerably, for example, bus fare, gasoline, car payments, babysitter costs, clothes, and uniforms.

Only one other secondary integration variable, church attendance, was consistently related to good mothercraft. Why this should be the case is not entirely clear. One can speculate that church ties are one type of social bond to community groups and strong social networks outside of the family. Sociological research has indicated that church attenders tend to be financially better off and older than nonattenders. Present data confirm these findings. Yet the relationship to good mothercraft was still strong even when we controlled for the effects of being better educated, urban, not in poverty, and older.

We found, in general, a positive relationship between social integration and quality of mothering. However, the impact of social integration as a strong mediating effect on poor mothercraft seemed to be negligible. The data clearly showed that poor socioeconomic conditions of the mother were the most important factor in the relationship between her mothering ability and the health of her child. These "structural" factors turned out to be more important than mediating ones such as familial and community integration.

In summary, we have seen that it is possible to evaluate objectively the quality of mothering given a young child. There is some validity to the measures of infant health—measures that reflect utilization of the health-care system. In this study, these measures were standards of preventive health care determined and agreed upon by medical professionals. In addition, a trained nurse's appraisal of the health of a child, based on taking a medical history and examining the physical condition of the child, was also related to mothercraft ability.

What did *not* appear to be related to mothercraft was the illness record of the child, the adequacy of the diet, or the weight-to-length ratio at 20 months. Poverty and low educational attainment were the factors that explained the illness record and diet, and being black was most highly related to obesity at 20 months.

When a relationship appeared between mothercraft and infant preventive health measures, we statistically controlled for the effects of poverty, poor education, and isolation. In almost every case, controlling for the effects of these items did not eliminate the relationship. What emerges, however, in this picture is a reflection of the complexities of life situations.

Poverty was related to low educational attainment. This in turn was reflected in poor health knowledge and understanding of the importance of preventive care. Poverty also implies greater chance of illness, which may require medical care of a nonpreventive nature.

Being situated in a family network in general appeared to provide a positive set of interactions for helping a mother raise a child. Yet we saw that these interactions were sometimes negative in content and affect. Ties outside the home such as to church, clubs, or work also appeared to have positive relationships to utilization of medical care.

Implications

What are the implications for health and community workers concerned with child development?

This research supports previous findings that socioeconomic constraints wreak havoc in some families and create situations that are beyond the control of the individuals involved (National Research Council 1976). National policies are recommended that will address the improvement of economic status of the poor. In the case studies presented here, we have seen that poor economic status often may mean poor housing, frequent moving, unstable household composition, and little constancy in income for food and clothing. Thus families in poverty, especially where the mother has not completed high school, should be targeted for extra attention. Such women are less likely to use preventive health services for their infants, and their children are more likely to experience more episodes of illness.

Second, the research has shown that women who are socially integrated, either by contacts with family, work, or social institutions, are more likely to have better mothercraft scores. For example, mothers who work may establish social ties to other institutions and often earn money that takes them out of the poverty class. Mothers living with extended relatives may obtain significant social and emotional support from these members. However, not all family ties produce positive inputs into a supportive network. We also learned that some mothers living with relatives found themselves overly burdened with additional unwanted responsibilities.

Nonetheless, it is reasonably safe to say that mothers who live alone with their child or children and do not work are likely to be socially isolated. Among these are women who may find mothering a burdensome, tedious, and unrewarding experience; they have few outlets for expressions of frustration, few offers of advice and counseling, and a general lack of adult conversation and communication.

Sue is one of our mothers who, although married, is socially isolated. She is very young, alone at home with two small children, and never goes to church or club activities. Her appraisal score worsened as time passed. Her husband leaves her alone a lot, and does not provide the kind of emotional and moral support she needs to cope with her babies. Her rural location also makes it more likely that she will not get necessary preventive medical care for her children. Clearly, she is an example of a mother who is socially isolated and should be marked for careful attention by health workers.

Third, although the concept of "inadequate mothering" can merge into the legal definition of "child neglect," little in the way of actionable child neglect was reported in this study. Why is this the case? It is not because child neglect does not occur. Of the twenty-five cases lost from the original 148 chosen for study, 11 were instances of actual or potential child neglect. The Division of Protective Services removed children from five homes and placed them in foster homes. In five other instances, the biological mother was unable or unwilling to care for the child and had handed over its care to a mother-surrogate (usually the maternal grandmother). The eleven cases constitute 7.4 percent of the original sample. This is roughly five times the proportion of children experiencing neglect, according to current Wisconsin estimates. [Although it is impossible to ascertain the prevalence of child neglect and abuse in the general population, experts estimate that approximately five cases of neglect occur to one of reported abuse (USDHEW National Center on Child Abuse and Neglect 1978, p. 13). In Wisconsin, 186 cases of abused children under 1 year of age were reported in 1977 (Oghalai 1978). The 5:1 ratio provides an estimate of 930 children out of approximately 64,000 children under the age of 1 who were neglected, or 1.4 percent. To be sure, this is a minimum estimate because of the underreporting of abuse. In any event, the rate of actual and potential neglect in our original sample (7.4 percent) is five times greater than the above general estimate (1.4 percent).]

Two conclusions can be drawn from the preceding statistics: (1) even within a purposive sampling frame, it is difficult to find cases of child neglect among a low-income population, and (2) in longitudinal studies that follow mother-child pairs, where the effects of parenting can be measured only after a certain passage of time, it is likely that the more overt and serious cases of neglect will drop out of the sample, either through societal controls that may remove the child from the damaging environment, or through personal control, where the mother removes herself from the care of the child.

Current thinking and policy about cases of child neglect is to try to maintain the family unit intact; that is, bolster its strengths, and provide assistance in improving its weaknesses (summarized in Hurt 1975, pp. 16–19). This research has indicated that in every home visited, there were, indeed, both positive and negative circumstances and stimuli. Having a community program that identifies mothers at risk of neglecting the care of their child is perhaps the first step. The instruments developed in this study may provide a start in aiding the process of early identification.

Second, a health visitor who checks in at the home of these previously identified mothers has a number of advantages. What may be of most importance is that the *family,* not only the mother-child pair, is the focus of attention. All members of the mother's household become important actors in the care of the newborn. Few communities, especially in rural areas, currently provide home services to families of newborns. This research, which used public health nurses as health visitors, has demonstrated the usefulness of repeated home visits to families needing guidance and help. Not only is the development and health of the infant checked, but the visits provide a number of other advantages. Some of these are:

1. The visit in the home of the mother allows her to be at ease in her own surroundings.
2. The home visit provides an opportunity for the health visitor to evaluate the home environment.
3. It provides an opportunity for the visitor to encourage the mother to continue positive behavior, remind her of activities or behaviors that had previously been discussed but not yet acted upon, and suggest new activities or behaviors that would benefit the mother-child relationship. Continuity of advice and patient education is established.
4. The visitor is able to provide the link between community resources and the family. Contacts can be established with required services when they are needed. For example, a nurse realized on one home visit that the baby had probably been exposed to lead poisoning; on the spot, she made an appointment for the baby to be screened at the lead clinic and arranged for a special carpool to convey mother and baby to the appointment.
5. The visitor can assess unmet needs of other members in the household and facilitate the receipt of the needed services. An example was the nurse's noticing a very young pregnant sister of the mother when making a home visit. The sister had just arrived from Mississippi and

had received no prenatal care. During the visit, the nurse made a prenatal appointment for the sister by telephone.

6. If the same visitor can return to make additional visits, rapport can be established between mother and healthworker. Once rapport is established, there is a chance of confidence developing, especially if the visitor is able to follow through on some proposed services. When the mother also follows through on some agreed-upon activity, then trust develops between them.

7. When a link is established between a community institution such as the nursing bureau and the family, there is a base established from which some coordination and integration of social and health services may take place. Too often there is a fragmented approach to obtaining services, especially when clients must go to individual specialized social-service agencies for every needed service. Concern about this fragmented situation has existed for many decades. Perhaps this home-health-visitor concept will alleviate some of the problems in this area.

The concept of the health visitor is a new one in the United States, although it has been utilized in Western Europe for many years. Kempe (1976) suggested that this visitor pay regular visits to homes of preschool children until the child attends school regularly. He feels the visitor would assist in early detection of child abuse, as well as provide valuable information about the household and its relationship to the health and development of the child. He envisions the role as one of a lay visitor, such as "successful, supportive, mature mothers acceptable to their communities" (Kempe 1976, p. 947) rather than a trained health professional.

Future Research

This book reports exploratory research. It answers some questions but raises others and suggests a number of avenues of investigation that should be followed.

First and perhaps most important, the mothercraft appraisal score and the various health measures should be tested on a broader population base. Because of the relative difficulty of finding poor-quality mothering, this research was targeted to a special population in two ways: Some screening of cases was performed for indicators of future mothering problems, and the sample was restricted to mothers living in relatively low-income neighborhoods. Poor mothering, without doubt, is found in all social classes. Therefore, if this measure of quality of mothercraft is to be thoroughly tested, the population should include middle-class families as well.

Second, the period under investigation in the infant's life should be lengthened. In the present study, for reasons outside the author's control (as explained previously), infants were followed from the ages of approximately 3 to 20 months. The 20-month cut-off was too early in the child's life for adequate testing of general physical, mental, and social development. Most of the motor skills that were tested at 20 months evolved from maturation processes. Social deprivation would have had to be severe for the progress of the developmental skills to have been significantly affected. Relatively few testable mental and social skills are developed between the twelfth and twentieth month, and thus there were very few chances to fail items in the Denver Developmental Screening Test, the test chosen to evaluate developmental progress in this study. The final visit and interview should be no earlier than the child's thirty-sixth month, and even better, the sixtieth month, when the child is preparing to enter school.

Third, the nutritional information obtained in the study should be expanded. A one-day, 24-hour recall apparently provides insufficient data for analyzing a small child's diet. The inconsistency of appetite and foods offered from day to day may be considerable. Perhaps a three-day recall, with the interviewer returning each day, might improve the quality of the data.

The obesity discovered in this study (3 out of 10 infants were at or above the ninetieth percentile in weight for length at 20 months) is astonishing and completely unexplained. There was no correlation with any part of the reported diet, nor with past records of height and weight of the child. In future research the height and weight of all members of the household should be obtained in order to evaluate a possible genetic component. Second, evidence of the activity level of the study child should be noted. And third, the diet record should probe in detail for food items that are easily overlooked such as high-calorie sugar water (Kool Aid), candy bars, soft drinks, butter, jelly, and jam.

Finally, it is advisable to choose a control group of mother-infant pairs who would be visited and interviewed only at the beginning and end of the study period, when the infants were 3 months and 60 months of age. This group would then provide a contrast with the study population on measures of infant health. In the present study, it was perhaps serendipitous that study families in trouble received more attention and visits from the nurses than families not having difficulties. Whereas this was helpful and necessary to the families concerned, it may have affected the research results. It is possible that the added attention and contacts with the problem families may have provided the links with medical institutions that were predicted to be lacking in this population. Therefore it is possible, but not provable, that the generally good levels of mental and physical development and of preventive medical care of the study babies may have been influenced by being included in the study.

An attempt was made to evaluate the impact of being in the study by having the nurses choose additional families from their files. These families lived in the same geographic area and had infants born about the same time as the study babies but had not had any nursing contact since the initial newborn routine visit. Twenty "control" families were matched on mother's age, race, and marital status with 20 study families. Details of the comparison are presented in appendix D. The conclusion from this small test was that there was little difference between the two groups of infants with respect to illness and accident experience of the babies or general development. However, the immunization records of the study babies were slightly better, and more social agencies were involved in assisting the study families compared with the control families. This provides some evidence to support our previous statement that being in the study provided certain links to the medical and social-welfare establishment and thus bridged the gap we predicted would exist with mothers in poverty.

Appendix A:
Wave 1 Interview Schedule and Mothercraft Appraisal

Project 10

Office Number_____

MOTHERCRAFT STUDY
(1974-1976)

Mother's First Name_____   Street Address_____

(Copy from Birth Certificate)

Infant's First Name_____   Sex of Infant ( ) Male
( ) Female
Date of Birth _____
Birthweight _____lbs. _____oz.   Length _____inches

SUMMARY RECORD

Date of	Baby's Age (months)	Baby's Weight (lbs)	Baby's Length (inches)	DDST
First Visit				
Second Visit				
Third Visit				

RECORD OF ALL CALLS

Nurse's Name	Address of Nurse	Record of Call (NAH, Ref., Int.)	Call Date	Time	Infant's Age

Race: ( ) Black   ( ) White   ( ) Other_____

You and your baby have been selected to participate in a study by the University of Wisconsin of the health needs of new mothers and their babies. The nurses of the _____ are helping to collect some information. I have some questions about you and your family which I would like to ask. First of all, who lives here in this household with you and your baby? Please tell me their relationship to you, first name, age, and sex. First let's start with the adults, then your children, oldest to youngest.

No.	Relationship to Respondent	First Name	Age	Sex
01	R ( )Mother ( )Other_____			
02	Study ( )Son Infant ( )Daughter			
03	Head (if ( )Husband not R) ( )Other_____			
04				
05				
06				
07				
08				
09				
10				
11				

1. Now, I have some questions about the baby's health. Has the baby been for a general physical checkup since you left the hospital?

    ( ) Yes   ( ) No

    1a. [IF YES] When was that? Date _____
                                        month/year

2. Has he/she received the baby shots (Diptheria, Tetenus, Whooping Cough Immunizations)?

    ( ) Yes   ( ) No   ( ) Yes, don't know which ones

3. Has he/she received the polio vaccine?

    ( ) Yes   ( ) No

4. Did the baby get any of the following illnesses since you left the hospital?

    4a. Colds   ( ) Yes   ( ) No
    4b. Diahrrhea   ( ) Yes   ( ) No
    4c. Rash   ( ) Yes   ( ) No
         [IF YES] Was it ( ) Diaper   ( ) Prickly heat
                           ( ) Other_____
    4d. Cough   ( ) Yes   ( ) No
    4e. Ear infection   ( ) Yes   ( ) No
    4f. Are there any illnesses I have not mentioned
         that _____ got since you left the hospital?   ( ) Yes   ( ) No
    4g. [IF YES TO 4f] What were they? _____
         _____

5. Has _____ had any accidents?   ( ) Yes   ( ) No
    5a. [IF YES] What happened? _____
         _____

6. Has _____ been in the hospital for any reason?   ( ) Yes   ( ) No
    6a. [IF YES] For what reason? _____
         _____

7. Has _____ been in the emergency room of a hospital?
                                                  ( ) Yes   ( ) No
    7a. [IF YES] For what reason?_____
         _____

8. Is the baby taking any medicines now?   ( ) Yes   ( ) No
    8a. [IF YES] Can you please tell me what they are for, what kinds of medicines, and who prescribed them?

         Type   Purpose   Prescribed by
         1._____
         2._____
         3._____

9. What is the baby eating now?

    ( ) Milk--breast fed   ( ) Cereal   ( ) Other _____

    ( ) Milk--SIMILAC, INFAMIL   ( ) Meat   _____

    ( ) Milk--evaporated   ( ) Vegetables   _____

10. Is your baby on a fairly regular schedule for eating?

    ( ) Yes → 10a. What is that? _____

    ( ) No

11. Is your baby on a fairly regular schedule for sleeping?

    ( ) Yes → 11a. In general what time does he awake? _____

                                                 a.m.

                11b. What time does he go to sleep for the night? _____

                                                         p.m.

    ( ) No

12. Now I have some questions about yourself. When was the last time you saw a doctor for a complete physical checkup when you had no symptoms of illness or injury?

    Date _____

          month/year

    ( ) Don't remember → 12a. Would you say it was ( ) in the past year

                                             ( ) 1-5 years ago

                                             ( ) 6-10 years ago

                                           ( ) More than 10 years ago

    ( ) Never

13. When was the last time you saw a doctor when you weren't feeling well?

    Date _____ → 13a. What was the problem?_____

          month/year

                                          _____

    ( ) Never

14. Have you had any of the following illnesses in the past 3 months?

14a.	Colds	( ) Yes	( ) No
14b.	Flu	( ) Yes	( ) No
14c.	Upset stomach	( ) Yes	( ) No
14d.	Bad headaches	( ) Yes	( ) No
14e.	"Nerves"	( ) Yes	( ) No
14f.	Insomnia (trouble sleeping)	( ) Yes	( ) No
14g.	Any others?	( ) Yes	( ) No
14h.	[IF YES] What were they?		

_____

15. Are you taking any medicines now?   ( ) Yes ( ) No

    15a. [IF YES] Can you tell me what kinds of medicine, what they are for, and who prescribed them?

          Type   Purpose   Prescribed by

        1. _____

        2. _____

        3. _____

16. Have you been in the hospital in the past three months outside of having the baby?

( ) Yes →16a. [IF YES] What was the problem? _____

( ) No

17. When was the last time you went to the dentist?

Date _____
     month/year

( ) Don't know, don't remember → 17a. Approximately how long ago was it? _____
                                                                              # years
( ) Never

18. When was the last time you had a Pap smear?

Date _____
     month/year

( ) Don't know, don't remember → 18a. Approximately how long ago was it? _____
                                                                              # years
( ) Never

19. I'm going to read a list of the way people sometimes feel. For each one, I'd like to know if, during the past few weeks, you felt that way many times, a few times, hardly at all, or never. During the past few weeks, did you ever feel . . .

[REPEAT THESE AFTER EACH QUESTION]

	Many times	A few times	Hardly at all	Never
19a. So restless that you couldn't sit long in a chair	( )	( )	( )	( )
19b. Very lonely or remote from other people	( )	( )	( )	( )
19c. Bored	( )	( )	( )	( )
19d. Depressed or very unhappy	( )	( )	( )	( )
19e. Upset because someone criticized you	( )	( )	( )	( )

20. Now I would like to ask you some questions about this last pregnancy. Was the baby born about when he/she was expected, or earlier, or later?

( ) Earlier than expected → 20a. About how early?
( ) When expected   ( ) Less than 4 weeks early
( ) Later than expected   ( ) 4 or more weeks early
( ) Don't know   ( ) Don't know

21. About how many months were you pregnant when you first went to the doctor?

_____ months

22. About how many times did you go to the doctor when you were pregnant?

_____ total number of prenatal visits

23. Where did you go for prenatal care? To a private doctor, a group of private doctors, a public clinic, an emergency room of a hospital, or someplace else?

( ) Private doctor → 23a. Was he a general practitioner or a specialist?
                          ( ) General Practitioner
                          ( ) Specialist
( ) Group of private doctors
( ) Public clinic
( ) Emergency room of a hospital
( ) Other → 23b. Specify _____
( ) No prenatal care

24. How many days did you stay in the hospital?   _____ days

25. Did the baby come home with you?

( ) Yes

( ) No → 25a. Please explain _____

_____

26. Were there any complications during this pregnancy?

( ) Yes → 26a. What was the trouble? _____

( ) No   _____

27. Were there any complications during birth?

( ) Yes → 27a. What was the trouble? _____

_____

( ) No

28. Did you go back to the doctor for a checkup after the baby was born? [POSTPARTUM CHECKUP]   ( ) Yes   ( ) No

29 Did you have insurance that covered:

29a. Your prenatal care?   ( ) Yes   ( ) No

29b. Your hospital costs?   ( ) Yes   ( ) No

30. Did you have any out-of-pocket expenses for:

30a. Your prenatal care?
     ( ) Yes → 30b. About how much? $_____
     ( ) No

30c. Your hospital costs?
     ( ) Yes → 30d. About how much? $_____
     ( ) No

31. When you were a child, did you go to the doctor regularly, not very often, or never?

( ) Regularly   ( ) Not very often   ( ) Never [GO TO Q. 32]

31a. Was this only when you were sick, for checkups as well as when you were sick, or just for checkups?

( ) When sick   ( ) When sick plus checkups   ( ) Just checkups

32. Did your family have one doctor that took care of everyone; one doctor for the children; no special doctor, they used many different ones; or no doctor at all?

( ) One doctor   ( ) One doctor   ( ) No special   ( ) No doctor
    for everyone   for children   doctor

33. What kind of medical person did your family use, a general practitioner, specialist, chiropractor, osteopath, faith healer, or someone else?

( ) General Practitioner   ( ) Osteopath
( ) Specialist   ( ) Faith healer
( ) Chiropractor   ( ) Other → 33a. Specify _____

34. Where were you usually taken for medical care, to a doctor's office, to an outpatient clinic, to an emergency room of a hospital, or someplace else?

( ) Doctor's office   ( ) Emergency room of hospital
( ) Outpatient clinic   ( ) Other → 34a. Specify_____

35. Would you say, as you think back, that you were basically a healthy child, sometimes healthy and sometimes sick, or almost always sick?

( ) Healthy child [GO TO Q. 36]
( ) Sometimes healthy, sometimes sick [ASK Q. 35a]
( ) Almost always sick [ASK Q. 35a]

35a. [IF R MENTIONS BEING SICK] What kind of sickness was it? _____
_____

36. Now I have some questions about you and your family. How many grades of school did you finish?

( ) Elementary or less (1 - 8)
( ) Some high school (9 - 11)
( ) High school graduate (12)
( ) Some college or post high school training
( ) College graduate

37. Did you work when pregnant with this baby?

( ) Yes ⟶   ( ) No ⟶

37a. What month did you stop working? _____(month) 37b. What was your job?	37c. Have you ever worked? ( ) Yes ( ) No 37d. What was your job?

38. Do you plan to work this coming year?

( ) Yes → 38a. Doing what? _____
( ) No

39. About how much was your family income in 1973? Here is a card showing amounts of weekly and yearly incomes. Next to each amount is a letter. Would you tell me what letter represents your income? [CIRCLE LETTER MENTIONED]

CARD 1

Weekly Income		Yearly Income	
A.	Under $20	AA.	Under $1,000
B.	20 - 38	BB.	1 - 1,999
C.	39 - 57	CC.	2 - 2,999
D.	58 - 77	DD.	3 - 3,999
E.	78 - 96	EE.	4 - 4,999
F.	97 - 115	FF.	5 - 5,999
G.	116 - 134	GG.	6 - 6,999
H.	135 - 154	HH.	7 - 7,999
I.	155 - 173	II.	8 - 8,999
J.	174 - 192	JJ.	9 - 9,999
K.	193 - 231	KK.	10 - 11,999
L.	232 - 288	LL.	12 - 14,999
M.	289 - 480	MM.	15 - 24,999
N.	480 or more	NN.	25,000 or more

40. Do you get any public assistance such as . . .

Food stamps	( ) Yes	( ) No
ADC or AFDC	( ) Yes	( ) No
Title 19 (Medicaid)	( ) Yes	( ) No
Unemployment compensation	( ) Yes	( ) No
Welfare (not further specified)	( ) Yes	( ) No
Other--Explain_____	( ) Yes	( ) No

41. What is your birthdate? _____
                            month/day/year

42. Where were you born? _____ city or county _____ state

43. How many brothers and sisters did you have when growing up?
    _____ brothers   _____ sisters

    43a. [IF ONE OR MORE] Were they older or younger?
         _____ younger brothers   _____ younger sisters
         _____ older brothers   _____ older sisters

44. How long have you lived in _____? _____ no. of years
                                   city or town

45. How long have you lived at this address? _____ no. of years

46. Are you now married, separated, divorced, widowed or single?
    ( ) Married [GO TO Q. 47,48,49]
    ( ) Separated [SKIP TO Q. 50]
    ( ) Divorced [SKIP TO Q. 50]
    ( ) Widowed [SKIP TO Q. 50]
    ( ) Single [SKIP TO Q. 50]

47. [IF MARRIED] How many grades of school did your husband finish?
    ( ) Elementary or less (1 - 8)
    ( ) Some high school (9 - 11)
    ( ) High school graduate (12)
    ( ) Some college or technical school
    ( ) College graduate

48. [IF MARRIED] What is the usual occupation of your husband? _____
    _____

49. [IF MARRIED] Is he currently employed, looking for work, retired or what?
    ( ) Employed → 49a. Is this ( ) full time
                             ( ) part time
    ( ) Looking for work
    ( ) Retired
    ( ) Other → 49b. Specify _____

50. What is your religious preference?
    ( ) Protestant → 50a. What denomination? _____
    ( ) Catholic
    ( ) Other ────→ 50b. Specify _____
    ( ) None

51. About how often do you usually attend religious services. Would you say, once
    a week or more, 2-3 times a month, once a month, a few times a year, or never?
    ( ) Once a week or more
    ( ) 2 - 3 times a month
    ( ) Once a month
    ( ) A few times a year, or less
    ( ) Never

52. One way in which some people spend their time is in clubs and organizations.
    Do you belong to any social clubs or organizations?
              ( ) Yes   ( ) No

53. How often do you go out for eating, drinking or seeing a movie? Would you say
     once a week or more, 2-3 times a month, a few times a year, or rarely, if ever?
     ( ) Once a week or more
     ( ) 2 - 3 times a month
     ( ) A few times a year
     ( ) Rarely, if ever

54. Do you read any newspapers regularly?
                    ( ) Yes   ( ) No

55. On the average, about how much do you watch TV? More than 2 hours a day, less
     than 2 hours a day, but daily, a few times a week, a few times a month, or
     rarely?
     ( ) More than 2 hours a day
     ( ) Less than 2 hours, but daily
     ( ) A few times a week
     ( ) A few times a month
     ( ) Rarely

56. How often do you get together informally with relatives or friends? Would you
     say once a week or more, 2-3 times a month, a few times a year, or rarely, if
     ever?
     ( ) Once a week or more
     ( ) 2 - 3 times a month
     ( ) A few times a year
     ( ) Rarely, if ever

57. Now I'd like to know how much experience you have had with babies.

		Little or none	Some	Great Deal
57a.	First, experience with babies around the house when growing up. Would you say none, a little, some, or a great deal?	( )	( )	( )
57b.	Reading about baby care	( )	( )	( )
57c.	Attending classes in prenatal care or care of the baby	( )	( )	( )
57d.	Babysitting with other people's babies	( )	( )	( )

58. Now, please tell me whether you think the following statements are true or false.

		True	False
58a.	A baby needs to be more warmly dressed than an adult.	( )	( )
58b.	It is good practice to prop a bottle so that a baby can feed himself.	( )	( )
58c.	Excitement can often cause a baby to spit up.	( )	( )
58d.	If a baby is fat, you know he is healthy.	( )	( )
58e.	The window in a baby's room should never be opened in the winter.	( )	( )
58f.	An overdosage of aspirin is a common cause of poisoning in children.	( )	( )
58g.	Some babies often spit up after all their feedings.	( )	( )

59. Do you think one person can catch these diseases from another?

		Yes	No	Don't know
59a.	Influenza	( )	( )	( )
59b.	Diabetes	( )	( )	( )
59c.	Allergies	( )	( )	( )
59d.	Measles	( )	( )	( )

60. If you need help or advice about your baby, are there people around to help?

    ( ) Yes → 60a. Who is that? _____
    ( ) No   (relationship to respondent)

61. Are there others who take care of your baby every day?

    ( ) Yes → 61a. Who is that? _____
    ( ) No   (relationship to respondent)

62. Some babies are easy to care for, others are more difficult--for example, they cry a lot, don't sleep very long, or you can't figure out how to make them happy. Would you say that _____, in general, is

    ( ) easy to care for or   ( ) more difficult to care for.

63. Now, please look at this picture. Tell me what looks wrong to you.

    [PROBE: What do you think could happen?]

    _____ Total number of items noted

64. Now I would like to ask you some questions about the number of children you had born alive altogether. Let's start with your first born.

   64a. What is his/her name?

   64b. When was he/she born?   [FILL IN BIRTH RECORD CHART BELOW]

   64c. A boy or a girl?

   Now the second child. [REPEAT 64a., 64b., 64c. FOR ALL LIVE BIRTHS]

65. Have any of your children died since birth?

   ( ) Yes → 65a. Which child(ren) was(were) that? When did he/she die?

   ( ) No   [FILL IN CHART]

66. Have you had any <u>pregnancies</u> that didn't result in a live birth?

   ( ) Yes → 66a. In what month and year did that pregnancy end? [FILL IN CHART]

             66b. How long had you been pregnant then? [FILL IN CHART]

   ( ) No

BIRTH RECORD CHART

Live Births

		1	2	3	4	5	6
64a.	Name						
64b.	Birthdate						
64c.	Sex						
65.	Date of Death						

Other Pregnancies

		1	2	3	4	5	6
66a.	Date of end of pregnancy if miscarriage or stillbirth						
66b.	Length of pregnancy (months)						

Continue on separate page for additional births or pregnancies.

67. Before this <u>last</u> pregnancy began, did you really want (a/another) child at some time?

   ( ) Yes
   ( ) No, didn't want another child
   ( ) Don't know, didn't care

68. Did you become pregnant sooner than you actually wanted, later than you wanted or just about the right time?

   ( ) Sooner
   ( ) Later
   ( ) Right time
   ( ) Don't know

69. Have you ever obtained any information about family planning from any doctor or agency?

   ( ) Yes → 69a. Who or where was that? _____
   ( ) No

70. Before you became pregnant this last time, did you ever use any method to delay
or prevent pregnancy?

( ) Yes   ( ) No [SKIP TO Q. 71]

70a. [IF YES] Here is a list of ways women sometimes delay or prevent pregnancies.
Please tell me the letter of all methods you have ever used. [SHOW CARD 2]

Letters mentioned ____ ____ ____ ____ ____ [IF "T" MENTIONED, SEE BELOW]

70b. [IF YES] Which one(s) were you using just before you got pregnant this last
time? [SHOW CARD 2]

Letters mentioned ____ ____ ____ ____ ____ [IF "T" MENTIONED, SEE BELOW]

70c. [IF YES] Had you stopped using this method before you became pregnant?

( ) Yes   ( ) No

71. Do you expect to have another child? Would you say definitely yes, probably yes,
probably no or definitely no?

( ) Definitely yes →
( ) Probably yes ⟶
( ) Uncertain ⟶

71a. How many children do you think you will have altogether?

_____ Total number

71b. About when do you expect to have your next child?

_____ months or _____ years

( ) Probably no
( ) Definitely no

CARD 2

A Pill
B Douche
C Foam
D Jelly, Cream, Suppository
E IUD, Coil, Loop
F Condom, Rubber
G Diaphragm
H Diaphragm and Jelly

J Rhythmn or safe period - Calendar
K Rhythmn or safe period - Temperature
L Not having intercourse to avoid
   pregnancy - abstinence
M Withdrawal, coitus interruptus
N Operation; sterilization - wife
P Operation; sterilization - husband
S Abortion
T Other _____

[ASK: What was that? FILL IN.]

	Agree	Disagree
Do you agree or disagree with the following statements?		
72. I have great faith in doctors.	( )	( )
73. As long as you feel all right, there is no reason to go to a doctor.	( )	( )
74. In general, I think doctors do a good job.	( )	( )
75. There is much a person can do to keep from becoming sick.	( )	( )
76. In general, I think most doctors are overrated.	( )	( )
77. If a person works at it he can stay in good health.	( )	( )
78. When there are colds going around, I am sure to get one no matter how much I try to avoid it.	( )	( )
79. I would rather not go to a doctor unless I have to.	( )	( )
80. Even if a person is not sick, he should see a doctor at least once a year for a routine checkup.	( )	( )
81. If you are going to get sick, you are going to get sick; no use worrying about it.	( )	( )

82. People go to see a doctor for different reasons. I'm going to describe a few symptoms and ask you whether or not you would consult a doctor if you had each of these problems.

		Yes	No	Don't Know
82a.	A temperature of 103° for two days	( )	( )	( )
82b.	A repeated sharp pain in your chest	( )	( )	( )
82c.	Severe cough and sore throat	( )	( )	( )
82d.	"Nerves"	( )	( )	( )
82e.	Frequent insomnia (sleeplessness)	( )	( )	( )
82f.	Unexplained weight loss	( )	( )	( )
82g.	Allergy	( )	( )	( )
82h.	Blood in your stools	( )	( )	( )
82i.	General fatigue (always tired)	( )	( )	( )

83. Do you think it is very important, somewhat important, or not important to take young children to a doctor for regular checkups even when they are feeling well?

( ) Very   ( ) Somewhat   ( ) Not

84. I'll read a list of symptoms children sometimes have. For each one please tell me whether or not you would consult a doctor if your child had the symptom.

		Yes	No	Don't Know
84a.	First, would you consult a doctor if the child seemed to be feeling poorly for several days and had a temperature of about 102?	( )	( )	( )
84b.	. . . seemed to have unexplained muscular aches or pains?	( )	( )	( )
84c.	. . . complained of a sore throat for three days but had no temperature?	( )	( )	( )
84d.	. . . the child had an earache?	( )	( )	( )

Thank you for your time. I would like to check back with you when your baby
is about a year old. May I have the name of someone who might know how to reach
you in case you move?

Name _____   Relationship_____

Address _____   Telephone_____

        _____

Name _____   Relationship_____

Address _____   Telephone_____

        _____

Office Number _____

Mother's Name _____

THUMBNAIL SKETCH OF INTERVIEW

General comments including: extent of previous contact w/family; problems w/interview (good, poor rapport); background information about R and family; (e.g. relationship of father of baby w/mother, w/baby; any chronic health conditions of mother; evidence that mother is/is not likely to seek medical care and/or follow nurse's advice for self/children; family problems)--

_____

_____

_____

_____

_____

_____

_____

_____

_____

_____

_____

_____

_____

_____

_____

_____

_____

_____

(Complete copies of Wave 2 and 3 interview schedules available upon request from author.)

Mothercraft Appraisal

Instructions

This set of ratings should be filled in immediately after the interview has been completed with the mother and child, never in the presence of the mother. There are various components of mothering that require an evaluation of characteristics of the interrelationship between mother and child that must be gleaned from careful observation. In addition, some factual components also must be evaluated on the basis of observation. Please do your best to check the yes or no category. Use the no-information category as sparingly as possible. If you wish to expand or modify the yes or no answer, write on the back of the sheet, identifying the items by number.

Scoring

On the original interview, the nurse was given the option of checking yes, no, or no information. On this copy we have inserted − 1 on each item to aid in scoring. That is, items were evaluated, and if the response indicated a negative condition, it was given the score of − 1. Thus positive responses and no information were treated the same and given a score of zero.

Add the checkmarks that correspond to the position of the − 1 on the mothercraft appraisal. For example, if the nurse checked yes on item 1, the score would be − 1. But if no or no information were checked, the score would be zero for item 1. The total score for the entire appraisal can range from 0 to − 60.

Components of Mothercraft

I.   Physical Environment
     A. Housing adequacy
     B. Safety and cleanliness
     C. Material attributes

II. Physical Needs of the Child
     A. Cleanliness and dress
     B. Rest
     C. Feeding
     D. Medical care

III. Emotional and Cognitive Care
   A. Handling
   B. Stimulation

IV. Personality of Mother
   A. Dependency scale
   B. Apathy-futility scale
   C. Verbal communication

	Scoring		
	Yes	No	No Information
I. *Physical Environment*			
A. *Housing Adequacy*			
1. Family lives mostly in one room in winter because of difficulty in heating entire house.	− 1		
2. Repairs one usually makes oneself are left undone.	− 1		
3. House is dilapidated; paint badly peeling, plaster broken; windows broken.	− 1		
4. Severe overcrowding.	− 1		
B. *Safety and Cleanliness*			
5. Gross uncleanliness in house: e.g., filth, old food scraps on floor or furniture.	− 1		
6. Flies, rodents, bugs present.	− 1		
7. Only one usable exit in and out of house.	− 1		
C. *Material Attributes*			
8. Table and chairs available to eat on.		− 1	
9. Furniture is obviously in need of repair.	− 1		
10. Living room doubles as bedroom.	− 1		
11. Family has at least one of the following: radio, stereo, TV, or record player.		− 1	
12. Child has toys of his own.		− 1	

	Scoring		
	Yes	No	No infor- mation

II. *Physical Needs of the Child*
  A. **Cleanliness and Dress**

	Yes	No	No information
13. Child unwashed for long periods.	− 1		
14. Child in dirty and/or ragged clothes.	− 1		
15. Evidence that child's underwear (diapers) is changed as needed.		− 1	
16. Child dressed inappropriately for weather.	− 1		

  B. *Rest*

	Yes	No	No information
17. Child has place for sleeping at bedtime away from family living and recreation space.		− 1	
18. A regular bedtime set for child.		− 1	
19. Child regularly gets less than 9 hours sleep most nights.	− 1		
20. Child has no routine time for arising.	− 1		

  C. *Feeding*

	Yes	No	No information
21. Child fed on flexible, but regular schedule.		− 1	
22. Child given food appropriate to age.		− 1	
23. Child fussy eater, "feeding problem."	− 1		
24. Child grossly overfed.	− 1		
25. Child grossly underfed. Hungry most of the day.	− 1		
26. Child fed meals with reasonably adequate nutrition appropriate for age.		− 1	

  D. *Medical Care*

	Yes	No	No information
27. Mother refuses or resists taking child for medical care after injury.	− 1		

		Scoring	
	Yes	*No*	*No infor-mation*
28. Neglect of obvious medical needs.	− 1		
29. Follows through on a medically prescribed treatment.		− 1	
30. "Insufficient concern" to report illness to helping person.	− 1		

III. *Emotional and Cognitive Care*
  A. *Handling*

31. Mother occasionally talks or croons to baby.		− 1	
32. Strokes or pats arm, hair, or other parts of baby's body.		− 1	
33. Picks up and holds baby with relative ease.		− 1	
34. Strained and tense when holding baby.	− 1		
35. Uses infant seat constantly.	− 1		
36. Only handles baby when necessary, e.g. to change diapers, location.	− 1		
37. Child is often ignored when he/she tries to get mother's attention.	− 1		
38. Mother is able to show physical affection to child comfortably		− 1	
39. Child is often pushed aside when he/she shows need for love.	− 1		

  B. *Stimulation*

40. Mother repeats "ma ma" or "da da" to child.		− 1	
41. Mother teaches simple sounds by repeating: "bow wow", water, bottle, baby, etc.		− 1	
42. Mother plays with child in simple way, e.g., rolls ball, grasps and pulls hands, peak-a-boo, etc.		− 1	

	Scoring		
	Yes	*No*	*No Information*

IV. *Personality of Mother*

   A. *Dependency Scale*

     43. Mother dwells on her problems with her child.   −1

     44. Clings to her children.   −1

     45. Frequently refers to opinions of or quotes her mother.   −1

     46. Keeps insisting that interviewer give advice or intervene on her behalf.   −1

   B. *Apathy-Futility Scale*

     47. Claims that she is unable to perform at job, or housework, or get anything done.   −1

     48. Hair is usually unkempt, tangled, or matted.   −1

     49. Clothes are usually dirty or in disarray.   −1

     50. From time to time becomes preoccupied or shows lapses of attention during conversation.   −1

     51. Has a sad expression or holds her body in a dejected or despondent posture.   −1

   C. *Verbal Communication*

     52. Speech is full of long pauses.   −1

     53. Speaks in a faint voice, or voice fades away at end of sentence.   −1

     54. Talks comfortably with interviewer by second contact.   (No) −1

     55. Talks in an ambiguous, obscure, vague, or cryptic manner.   −1

     56. Answers questions with single words or by phrases only.   −1

     57. Talks of her situation with practically no outward sign of emotion.   −1

	Scoring		
	Yes	*No*	*No Information*
58. Shows warmth in voice much of time with interviewer.		−1	
59. Shows warmth in tone in discussing her children.		−1	
60. Keeps eyes closed or averted.	−1		

Appendix B:
Surrogate Cases

Five of the original mothercraft study babies came under the care of a surrogate mother after the beginning of the study. Three of the surrogate mothers were foster parents selected by the county, and the other two were the maternal grandmothers of the children. In four of these cases the biological mother was the primary caretaker at the first interview, and then another woman assumed responsibility for the child. In the fifth instance, the surrogate mother did not assume care until after the second interview took place with the mother.

Several similarities appear in these five cases: The biological mothers were unmarried, young when their first child was born, came from large families within minority-group subcultures, and generally gave some early evidence of problems with mothering. But each case also has many individual characteristics, and so some of the details of each situation are described here. The first four cases come from the urban area of the study, and the fifth from a small urban area in rural Wisconsin. Of course, all names used in these sketches are fictional.

Mary and Infant Kathy

Mary was born in Mississippi but, as an infant, was sent to live with her aunt and uncle in Michigan, who raised her until she was 14. She likes her aunt very much and expresses resentment at her mother for giving her up, although her mother had too many children to be able to care for them properly. She then moved to Milwaukee to live with her mother, after her step-uncle allegedly sexually abused her. There she completed the ninth grade while often being truant and was sent to a state school for delinquent girls after running away. She was sent there several times and eventually to a state prison for women where her first child, Tommy, was born in 1968 when she was 19. Tommy was removed from her care by the Department of Public Welfare, and Mary's mother now has legal custody of the child.

A daughter, Sara, was born in 1973, and after noting the lack of adequate physical and emotional care, the public health nurse found her a place in a Montessori day school where she seemed to be doing very well.

Mary never used any form of contraception and became pregnant again about 4 months after the birth of Sara. Kathy, born in October of 1974, had the same father as Sara. The father was described as a heavy drinker who physically abused Mary but never harmed the children.

169

The nurse chose this case because of the poor mothering capabilities that had continually been in evidence. She noted that Mary's self-image seemed to be very low; she was overweight, poorly groomed, had never been married, and had a troubled background.

At the first interview in December of 1974, the study baby, Kathy, was not quite 2 months old. Mary was 26 years old. The household also included Sara, her 15-month-old daughter. They were living in a rundown flat in the central-city area. The mother had not initiated prenatal care for this last pregnancy until she was 6½ months pregnant, and Kathy was delivered weighing 5 lb, 14 oz. Mary was not working and received ADC, food stamps, and medicaid with a total 1973 income of $3000 to $3999. She was an active church member where she played the organ for services.

At the second interview, Kathy, the study baby, was 10 months old, and her weight was extremely low. She had been hospitalized earlier for failure to gain weight and for diarrhea. The mother continued to have severe problems in providing proper physical and emotional care to her daughters in spite of extensive nursing and social-service-worker involvement.

In October of 1975, both girls were removed from their mother's care by Protective Services and placed first in separate temporary receiving homes and then together in a foster home. Mary could not be located by the nurse from October of 1975 until April of 1976 when the nurse reported that she was working full time as a power machine operator. She was living in pleasant surroundings with a different man whom she planned to marry and had hopes of getting her children back eventually. She had made arrangements to visit the children and had realized that she had not been able to take proper care of them in the past. The nurse reported that she "feels that Mary had become more mature and that perhaps some day she may be able to be a 'good mother' and/or find success in some other area of endeavor."

The third interview was conducted with the foster mother when the study child was 18 months old. The foster parents were a couple in their fifties who had never had children of their own. Kathy's weight was now in the normal range, and both girls were doing very well by all indications.

Mary's mothercraft appraisal score was −27 at wave 1 and −31 at wave 2. The foster mother's score was 0 at wave 3.

Anita and Infant Michelle

Anita was born in Tennessee, one of ten children, and moved to Milwaukee with her family when she was 8 years old. She became pregnant for the first time when she was 13. Her family did not know of the pregnancy until the seventh month. She then started seeing a doctor and attended a special school for young mothers where she received training in prenatal and infant care. Anita's daughter, Michelle, was delivered two weeks before Anita's fourteenth birthday. Michelle weighed 5 lb, 6 oz. at birth.

At the first interview, Anita and Michelle were living with Anita's divorced mother, Carol, age 53, and two of Anita's brothers. Anita expressed some depression to the nurse, saying that she was having problems in school and was gaining weight now that she was taking birth-control pills. Anita was also taking some unprescribed diet pills. The nurse advised her on the dangers of these. The nurse also discussed her adjustment to caring for Michelle and noted that Anita depended quite a bit on her mother to care for the baby but that Anita did not want to admit this.

At the time of the second interview Carol had complete responsibility for Michelle's care. Anita would come home only to change clothes, no longer living there because her mother would not let boys stay overnight with her. Carol expressed a lot of worry about Anita's frequent truancy from school and unknown living place. Carol was providing good care and affection to Michelle but seemed burdened by having to care for a baby when she thought she had finished that stage of her life.

Michelle was 19 months old at the third interview and still living with Carol, her grandmother, and her youngest son, Michelle's uncle, the same situation as the second interview. Carol continued to give Michelle good care but continued to worry about Anita who had changed her plans to return to school. This led the nurse to state that Carol was accepting the situation with quiet resignation.

Anita was living with her boyfriend in Chicago and had had Michelle with her for a month during the time between the second and third interviews. She delivered a second daughter in Chicago shortly before the third interview took place with Carol. She then visited Carol with Michelle and her newborn daughter, leaving Michelle there and returning to her unknown residence in Chicago. The nurse felt that these changes were hard on Michelle, and the emotional climate in Carol's home had suffered.

Anita's mothercraft appraisal score at wave 1 was -17; Anita's mother, Carol's, mothercraft appraisal score was -9 at wave 2 and -3 at wave 3.

Alice and Infant Gloria

Alice came from a family of eight children and had spent much of her childhood in a foster home because her mother neglected her. Her first child, Connie, was born before Alice's sixteenth birthday and her second child, a son, was born less than 10 months later. Because this baby was very small and required a lot of special care, Alice gave him up for adoption. The study baby, Gloria, was born when Alice was 20 years old. She was living in her family's home but soon moved out because she did not like the situation there: her brothers and sisters would hit Connie, smoke dope, and have a lot of people in the house.

Alice moved in with her boyfriend's mother, Viola (age 38), and her 15-year-old son, and was living there at the time of the first interview. Alice's boyfriend—Gloria's father—was going to college in another city but planned to continue his education in Milwaukee after their planned marriage. Alice and Viola did not always get along well, and Alice felt lonely except when her boyfriend was home on the weekends. She stated that all she wanted was to get married and be happy. The nurse noted that Alice showed much delight in both her children and gave them good care.

Between the first and second interview, Alice's home situation changed. She never married Gloria's father but met another man who promised to marry her. He could not stand Gloria's crying so Alice had her placed in a foster home and then got married. The newly married couple tried living with Gloria again for 8 days but returned her to the foster mother because of the crying. At the second interview, Alice told the nurse that she was planning to separate from her husband.

The second interview took place in the foster home when Gloria was 1 year old. Her foster parents were a couple in their fifties who had a grown son and a 12-year-old daughter at home. They gave Gloria a lot of attention and good care.

At the third interview Gloria, now 19 months, was still in the foster home. She had spent two weekends with her mother since the second interview. The nurse characterized the foster mother as pleasant, happy with Gloria, and concerned about getting information on her immunization history so that it could be continued. The nurse also noted that Gloria did not have other children her own age to play with and that the foster mother, due to her age, probably did not have the energy to play a lot with Gloria.

Alice's mothercraft appraisal score at wave 1 was -4; the foster mother's score was -1 at wave 2 and -2 at wave 3.

Janice and Infant John

Janice's first child, Louis, was born when she was 15 years old, followed by Tammy a year later, and by John, the study baby, one more year later when Janice was 17. At the time of the first interview, she was living alone with her three children, receiving public assistance to support her family. The nurse stated that her rapport with Janice was poor, in contrast with a previous visit she had made. Janice gave vague and often conflicting answers to the nurse's questions. The nurse felt that Janice gave good physical care to her children but that the emotional environment was somewhat poor and that Janice seemed overwhelmed by her responsibility.

At the time of the second interview, John, 14 months, was living with his maternal grandmother, Rita (age 35), three of her children (ages 12, 11, 7), and three more of her grandchildren (ages 4, 3, 2), including Janice's other two children. Rita was separated from her husband, but occasionally he would babysit for the children. Rita had legal custody of John and stated that "Janice never wanted kids, didn't take care of them and so she gave them to me." Rita seemed glad to have nursing service available and impressed the nurse with her intelligence, energy, and determination. She had plans for the children's medical care and expressed concern that John had not been talked to enough. The nurse learned that Janice was "around" sometimes, but gave no care to the children, and Rita felt she had previously neglected them.

The home situation was the same at the third interview, except that Rita's husband was again living with her. He took care of the children at times, and John seemed to be doing very well. The nurse reported that Rita had untreated hypertension and seemed nervous, but the nurse felt that John was lucky to be with this family rather than with his mother. Rita said she was ashamed of Janice's behavior. Janice visited John about once a month for ten minutes.

Janice's mothercraft appraisal score at wave 1 was −27; Rita's score was 0 at wave 2, and −2 at wave 3.

Judy and Infant Brian

Judy was one of eleven children born to an American Indian mother and a white father. Her family was known to the nursing agency because of frequent contacts concerning inadequate care of the children. Judy's son, Brian, was born when she was 17, and they lived in her parents home, a city of 18,000, for a short time after his birth. They then moved to a small apartment and Judy returned to high school.

Brian was almost 6 months old at the time of the first interview. Judy had taken him to the doctor since birth but wanted the nurse to reassure her that he was healthy. The nurse felt that she was warm and affectionate with Brian but was also immature and often regarded him as a toy or cute, playful object. Judy spoke of plans to marry her boyfriend within the year and also of feelings of boredom and depression. She liked to have people around, and her brother, his girlfriend, and her boyfriend visited her very often. Judy gave permission to the nurse to interview the babysitter who cared for Brian while she was in school but only could give the nurse the woman's first name and telephone number.

The nurse visited Brian's babysitter, a young, competent mother of three children and from her heard a different story of the care Judy was giving to Brian. The babysitter felt that Brian was poorly fed, saying that

Judy sent only cereal and Kool Aid for his food. She believed Judy's instructions to limit his nap to one-half hour were because Brian would not sleep at night due to hunger and not due to longer naps as Judy believed. When the babysitter gave specific instructions to Judy, they were followed, but she felt that Judy was unsure of herself and needed more training in child care. The nurse made plans to follow Brian's diet more carefully as a result of this visit.

As a result of nursing and social-worker evaluations, Brian was removed from Judy's care and placed in a foster home. The second interview took place there when Brian was 1 year old. The foster parents were a couple in their late thirties with five children of their own, ranging in age from 16 to 10. Betty, the foster mother, who had some Indian heritage, had been a foster child herself and felt strongly the need to give her own children, and Brian, a warm and secure home. The nurse felt that Brian was well stimulated and cared for in his foster home. Judy had visited him twice but was now living in Milwaukee.

Brian was in the same foster home at the time of the third interview. Betty had a 3-year-old foster child as well, and the rest of her family remained the same. Judy had visited Brian once, and Betty felt she completely ignored him otherwise, forgetting him on holidays. Betty was upset that Judy had written to the social-service department with a request to return to the county, get Brian back, and receive financial aid; Betty felt this request was made solely for the income. The nurse reported that Brian was well cared for and given good medical care and had become a delightful child.

Judy's mothercraft appraisal score at wave 1 was − 7; foster mother's score was 0 at wave 2, and − 1 at wave 3.

Appendix C:
An Evaluation
of Component Items
in Mothercraft
Appraisal Score

Test of Reliability of Mothercraft Appraisal Score

A test of reliability was made during the period of the second interview. This component was designed to answer the question of whether two observers rate mothers in the same way on the mothercraft appraisal score, given the same situation to observe.

With the cooperation of the Bureau of Nursing in Milwaukee, ten supervisors were asked to accompany ten nurses on three of their home visits. This meant that 30 babies and mothers were visited by a team of two nurses. After the visit, each nurse filled in the appraisal form independently, without communicating with the other. This resulted in having two appraisal ratings for 30 babies, one from the nurse, the other from the nurse supervisor.

This procedure pointed up two distinct problems:

1. The identification of items that nurses had difficulty rating (items that nurses would check "no information")
2. The identification of those items on which the ratings of the nurse and the supervisor did not agree

1. Taking items that nurses had the greatest difficulty rating: Out of 78 items, for supervisors, there were 16 items where over one third of the homes could not be rated. (Only 2 items were this serious a problem for the nurses.) These items were primarily in the rating of housing condition: heating problems (the second-wave interviews were conducted in the summer months), and absence of knowledge as to whether books, toys, and toilet paper were in the home. Another area that the supervisors found difficult to rate were items pertaining to the mother's relationship with the husband or father. Supervisors did not have the familiarity with the families as the nurses did from previous contacts.

2. Items that were rated by both the nurse and supervisor but on which the rating did not agree: In general, the range of agreement for the 78 items ranged from 44 to 100 percent. The mean percent of agreement was 87.6 percent. Only 8 items dropped below 75 percent agreement.

There appeared to be three problem areas:

1. Evaluation of home-environment conditions, for example, whether the house was dilapidated or whether there was gross uncleanliness in home (items 3, 5; see appendix A).
2. Verbal stimulation: whether mother repeats "mama" to child or teaches simple sounds (items 40, 41).
3. Verbal communication of mother. Items such as "speech full of long pauses, answers questions with single words" (items 52, 56).

Common Denominator Score

After the study was completed, a thorough analysis was performed to see if there were certain items that the nurses were consistently not able to answer. In addition, items that the nurse supervisors had difficulty with in the reliability study were also taken into account. A common denominator score was calculated at each wave. It contained 60 items and was obtained as follows:

Starting with 78 items in the first wave, 13 items were dropped because at least 10 percent of the time they were not able to be rated by the nurses or the interrater reliability was low. Examples of items dropped because of nurse's inability to judge were:

Child receives special attention when he/she is sick or feeling poorly. (Nurse often did not see mother when child was sick.)

There are some books in home (Nurse did not see any in living or dining room but did not see what was in bedroom).

Roof or pipes leak. (Nurse had no way of observing this unless it was raining or had rained, or she was in room where leak occurred.)

One item was dropped because of ambiguity of interpretation ["Readily lets another woman (mother, sister) take over care of baby"], and four items were dropped because they did not appear on all three waves or did not apply to all mothers. For example, "Clings to her husband in fearful, dependent way" could not be rated for mothers who did not have husbands.

The mothercraft appraisal score, consisting of ratings by the public health nurses is the major measure of quality of mothercraft. After eliminating some items for inappropriateness, ambiguity, and poor rating responses, a total of 60 items remained that were rated at three points in time. This 60-item checklist was then used for calculating the value of the mothercraft appraisal score (MAS) in this book.

Appendix D:
An Experimental-
Control Test of Effects
of Participation in Study

The purpose of this analysis was to find out whether family participation in the mothercraft study may have affected the health and development of the study infant in any way. That is, is there evidence that the babies who were followed for 17 months by public health nurses in the mothercraft study had medical histories or health measurements that differ from similar babies who did not participate in the study.

In order to investigate this problem, the Bureau of Public Health Nursing, City of Milwaukee, agreed to participate in a control sample study. The same geographic areas used in the original study were included. Nurses who had *not* participated in the mothercraft study were asked to search their files for babies born June-August 1974 and with whom they had not had any contact since the initial newborn routine visit. They were provided with a two-page form, the first page requesting information about the household composition and some demographic information about the mother; the second about the health and medical history of the child. Records for 20 families and babies were obtained from 9 nurses. Because of the comparatively homogenous geographic areas in Milwaukee, families with socioeconomic resources similar to the mothercraft families were obtained.

Procedure

In order to compare the control babies with the mothercraft babies, the 20 control mothers were matched with 20 mothercraft mothers by age, race, and marital status. Using data from the first interviews, perfect matches were made for about 10 mothers. For the remainder, matching was nearly impossible, particularly in regard to age of the mother. However, mothercraft mothers who were closest in age to the control mothers were chosen. Race of mother was matched in 19 of the cases.

Data obtained included basic information on mother, infant, and household composition. A medical history of the child, nurse's health appraisal of the child and DDST were included, as well as the Department of Health, Education, and Welfare growth-chart information.

Results

Infant's Sex, Race, and Age

There was essentially no difference in the variables of sex, race, and age of the two sets of infants. The control group contained 9 boys and 11 girls—the mothercraft group, 8 boys and 12 girls. There were 8 black, 10 white, 1 black-white, and one Indian-Arabian control babies; 9 black and 11 white study babies. In both groups the majority of children were born between June and August of 1974 making them all approximately the same age—between 18 and 23 months when examined.

Birthweight

There was a difference in the birthweight between the controls and the study babies, with the range of the controls from approximately 2 lb to 10 lb, and the mothercraft babies from 5 lb to 9 lb. Even without considering the 2-lb baby (who was 3 months premature), the mean weight of the study babies was somewhat heavier. At the time of the interview, the mothercraft babies had a mean weight of about 28 lb, the controls a mean weight of 26 lb. The mean height for both groups was approximately 32 in. Although the study babies were somewhat heavier, they were not proportionately taller. The mean head circumference was approximately 48 cm for both groups.

Immunizations

Immunization data were obtained from both the mother's report and the Bureau of Nursing records. The two groups were similar in the immunizations they had received, particularly DPT and polio. Half the babies, 10 of each group, had received 3 DPT inoculations, and 6 of the controls and 7 of the study babies had received the booster as well; only 2 controls and 1 of the study babies had received no DPT immunization, 2 of each group had 2 inoculations in the series. The similarities continue with the polio immunization data having exactly the same distribution as the DPT. However, frequencies for Rubella (measles) show a difference between the groups. Of the controls, 8 babies had not had the immunization, 12 had; of the study babies only 2 had *not* received the immunization and 18 had. This finding may reflect the influence on the mothercraft mothers of the regular visits and advice from the nurses. The distribution of those receiving other immunizations such as mumps and smallpox was exactly the same. Sixteen of the 20 in both groups had received no other immunizations.

Medical Histories

The mothers were asked several questions to obtain as complete a medical history as possible for each baby. They were asked whether there had been any occurrence of several specific conditions (lead poisoning, asthma, pneumonia, seizures, otitis media, allergy), then asked what communicable diseases the child had contracted and whether the child had any illness, injury or surgery. The combination of all responses to these questions yielded 17 different illness conditions, three accidents, and no surgery in either the control group or study group.

One accident was reported in the control group and was determined not to be serious. The two accidents in the study group were more serious: one child lost three teeth and the other suffered an electrical shock. As shown in table D-1, the study group had more occurrences of seven conditions, and the controls had more occurrences of five conditions. The remaining five conditions occurred equally in both groups. Also in both groups about one fourth of the infants had two or more conditions mentioned in their medical histories.

Table D-1
Medical Conditions during First Twenty Months of Life

Condition	Study Group	Control Group
Otitis media	5	9
Accidents	2	1
Allergies	3	1
Colds	0	2
Seizures	1	0
Lead poison	1	0
Whooping cough	1	0
Inward foot rotation	1	0
Failure to thrive	1	0
Cellulitis	1	0
Pneumonia	1	1
Chicken pox	1	1
Earaches	1	1
Anemia	1	1
Bronchitis	1	1
Conjunctivitis	0	1
Kidney problem	0	1
Congenital hip displacement	0	1

Nurse's Health Appraisal of Infant

The nurse's health appraisal, which listed 19 physical areas the nurse checked for problems or unusual conditions, showed differences between the two groups on 9 items. On each point there was usually not more than one case in either group with any problem except for three areas: Three mothercraft babies had a problem with posture or extremities as compared with 2 control babies, 2 mothercraft babies had loco-coordination trouble whereas none of the controls had this problem; and 3 study babies had dental problems compared with 2 controls. The mothercraft subjects had more cases with more than one problem area than did the controls. Seven of the control babies had one problem area, 13 had none; 3 of the study babies had one problem, 1 had two problems, and 1 had five problem areas—15 study babies had none.

The nurse also evaluated eating, sleeping, toilet habits, and personal hygiene of the babies and noted any problems in these areas. Five of the control babies had negative comments written about eating habits compared with 3 study babies with problems. Sleep and toilet habits were exactly the same for both groups, each having one case with a negative comment from the nurse. Personal hygiene was a problem area for 3 controls, while the study babies had no negative comments on that aspect of health. In summary, on two of these four points the controls did not do as well as the study babies, and on two points both groups were the same.

When these four areas were summed for each baby, the study babies were better off. Seventeen had no problems, 2 had one problem, and 1 had three problem areas. The controls had 12 cases problem free, 6 cases with one problem each, and 2 cases with two problems. Thus more of the controls had at least one problem.

At the end of the health appraisal, the nurse assigned a score of (1) excellent, (2) good, (3) fair, or (4) poor based on her judgment of the child's overall health status. As shown in table D–2, the control group generally received higher ratings. The mean score shows the overall health-status rating of the control infants to be slightly higher than the study group.

Denver Developmental Screening Test

DDST tests were given to all children and scored in the conventional manner of expecting a pass on all items that have been passed by 90 percent of all children at that particular age. With this scoring, one of the control babies was abnormal, but all the mothercraft babies passed. Neither group had delays in personal/social items. There was one case of delay in both fine-motor/adaptive and gross-motor items in the control group while

Table D–2
Infant's Health Status as Rated by Nurse

Rating	Study Group	Control Group
Excellent (1)	6	11
Good (2)	10	6
Fair (3)	4	3
Poor (4)	0	0
Total	20	20
Mean	1.9	1.6

mothercraft babies had no delays on those items, but did have one case of one delay in language while the controls had no delays in that area.

When rescored at a 75-percent level of passing, the controls had one questionable and one abnormal case, and the study group had only one questionable case. The items that seem to be problems for the controls, fine-motor/adaptive and gross motor, again showed up with more delays, and the study babies still had more language delays than the controls.

Weight, Length, and Weight for Length

The birthweight, and weight, length, and weight for length at the time of the nurse's visits were recorded on the DHEW growth charts (National Center for Health Statistics 1977b). Direct comparisons between the two groups were possible because charting was done by age of child. The study babies were heavier at birth (see table D–3), their median weight being in the fiftieth percentile while the median for the controls was in the eleventh to twenty-fifth percentile. Four study babies were on or above the ninety-fifth percentile, whereas only one control baby was this heavy at birth.

At the time of the nurse's visit, when the babies were 18 to 23 months old, the study babies continued to be heavier for their age but not longer. The median length for age for the study group was between the eleventh and twenty-fifth percentiles, and for the control group, the twenty-sixth and fiftieth percentiles, as can be seen in table D–4. Although more control babies fell into the extreme group below the fifth percentile in length, more study babies were at or below the twenty-fifth percentile and thus accounted for the slightly shorter length for age of this group.

Weight for age at this time showed a wider range for the control group, whose median weight was slightly above the fiftieth percentile (see table D–5). The study-group median was between the seventy-fifth and eighty-

Table D–3
Birthweight as Growth-Chart Percentiles

Percentile	Study Group	Control Group
On or below 5th	1	2
6th to 10th	2	2
11th to 25th	3	7
26th to 49th	1	1
50th	5	3
51st to 74th	2	2
75th to 89th	2	1
90th to 94th	0	1
On or above 95th	4	1
Total	20	20
Median	50th percentile	11th–25th percentile

Table D–4
Length for Age

Percentile	Study Group	Control Group
On or below 5th	3	5
6th to 10th	2	1
11th to 25th	5	1
26th to 49th	3	5
50th	0	2
51st to 74th	2	1
75th to 89th	2	2
90th to 94th	1	2
On or above 95th	2	1
Total	20	20

ninth percentiles. Half the control babies were at or below the fiftieth percentile in weight while only 3 of the study babies were recorded there. Five of the study babies were at or above the ninety-fifth percentile; three controls were.

As would be expected, the study babies were higher in the weight-for-length percentiles as well (see table D–6): The median was the ninetieth percentile for them and just about the seventy-fifth percentile for the controls. Again the distribution of the controls was greater, with more cases

Table D–5
Weight for Age

Percentile	Study Group	Control Group
On or below 5th	0	1
6th to 10th	0	0
11th to 25th	2	3
26th to 49th	0	3
50th	1	3
51st to74th	5	4
75th to 89th	4	1
90th to 94th	3	2
On or above 95th	5	3
Total	20	20

Table D–6
Weight for Length

Percentile	Study Group	Control Group
On or below 5th	0	2
6th to 10th	0	1
11th to 25th	1	2
26th to 49th	1	1
50th	0	2
51st to 74th	2	1
75th to 89th	6	3
90th to 94th	2	1
On or above 95th	8	7
Total	20	20

appearing at the low end of the scale and more study babies above the seventy-fifth percentile.

Community Agencies Serving the Families

The two groups differed in the number and type of community agencies active in the home. Eight mothercraft families listed agencies working with them: five families mentioned one agency, three families had contact with two agencies. Seven control mothers mentioned agencies: six families had one agency active, and one family had two agencies involved. More mothercraft families had contact with public health nurses (6) than did the controls (1), who instead had more contact with the Department of Public Welfare. More study mothers listed a second agency active in the home than did the controls.

Summary

The control and study babies were surprisingly similar. They were distributed in similar proportions by sex, age, race, and birthweight except that there was one premature infant included in the controls. Both groups had the same proportion immunized against DPT, polio, mumps, and small pox. However, the study babies had a greater proportion immunized against Rubella.

Most items in the medical history showed little difference between groups with respect to various illnesses and numbers of accidents, although there was more potentially serious illness reported in the study group. The nurse's appraisals of the infant's physical condition and general health patterns indicated about the same proportion of negative ratings, although the specific problems varied. DDST scores were similar, but one control group baby scored very poorly.

Several of the minor differences between these two groups could be ascribed to the differences in amount of nursing contact. The control-group families had not been visited by a public health nurse since shortly after the baby's birth. On the other hand, all the study families had been visited three times after the initial newborn visit, and almost half had been visited more often. Thus the nurses working with the study families knew much more of the babies' health histories and could elicit more accurate responses to the health questions. In addition, the nurse's knowledge probably enabled her or him to more accurately rate the child's overall health status.

The study babies were somewhat heavier in weight from birth to the examination date, and this was also reflected in the weight-for-length scores. The nurse's overall health ratings for the infants were slightly better for the control group than the study group.

The study families were reported as having more contacts with other social agencies, especially multiple agencies in one family. More contact with the Bureau of Nursing was reported for study families, and more contacts with the Department of Public Welfare for the control families.

There are two more dramatic differences that emerge from this analysis: (1) More study babies were immunized against Rubella, and (2) more social agencies were involved with study families as compared with control families. Both of these items could be interpreted as due to the involvement of public health nurses in the lives of the study families during their participation in the study. The greater proportion of children immunized against Rubella is likely due to the encouragement by the nurse for the parent to obtain the immunization.

It is also likely that the nurse had established rapport with the mother during the course of the study so that the family now has a personal link to the well-baby medical system. It is not unreasonable to assume that the greater knowledge the study nurse may have of the problems and needs of the study family may lead to the nurse's making appropriate referrals and contacts with other helping agencies in the city.

References

Aday, Lu Ann, and Ronald Andersen. 1975. *Development of Indices of Access to Medical Care.* Ann Arbor, Mich.: Health Services Administration Press.

Anderson, Ronald. 1968. *A Behavioral Model of Families' Use of Health Services.* Research Series 25. Chicago, Ill.: Center for Health Administration Studies.

Andrews, Frank; J. Morgan; J. Sondquist; and L. Klem. 1973. *Multiple Classification Analysis.* Second edition. Ann Arbor: University of Michigan, Institute for Social Research.

Baldwin, Wendy. 1976. "Adolescent pregnancy and childbearing: Growing concerns for americans." *Population Bulletin* 31:3–34.

Barry, H., and Barry, H., Jr. 1967. "Birth order, family size and schizophrenia." *Archives of General Psychiatry* 17:435.

Beal, V.A. 1967. "The nutritional history in longitudinal research." *Journal of the American Dietetic Association* 51:426–432.

Beck, M.B. 1970. "Abortion: The mental health consequences of unwantedness." *Seminars in Psychiatry* 2:263–274.

Becker, Marshall, and L. Green. 1975. "A family approach to compliance with medical treatment: A selective review of literature." *International Journal of Health Education* 18: 2–11.

Becker, Marshall H., and Lois A. Maiman. 1975. "Sociobehavioral determinants of compliance with health and medical care recommendations." *Medical Care* 13 no. 1 (January): 10–24.

Beverstock, Frances, and Robert P. Stuckert, eds. 1972. *Metropolitan Milwaukee Fact book: 1970.* Milwaukee, Wis.: Milwaukee Urban Observatory.

Bice, Thomas W., and Esko Kalimo. 1971. "Comparisons of health-related attitudes: A cross-national factor analytic study." *Social Science and Medicine* 5:283–318.

Brown, G.W., and Rutter, M. 1966. "The measurement of family activities and relationships." *Human Relations* 19:241–263.

Bullough, Bonnie. 1972. "Poverty, ethnic identity and preventive health care." *Journal of Health and Social Behavior* 13 (December): 347–359.

Charney, E.; H.C. Goodman; M. McBride; B. Lyon; and R. Pratt. 1976. "Childhood antecedants of adult obesity." *New England Journal of Medicine* 295:6–9.

Christy, R., ed. 1972. *Standards of Child Health Care.* Evanston, Ill.: American Academy of Pediatrics.

David, H. 1971. "Mental health and family planning." *Family Planning Perspectives* 3 no. 2:20–23.

Denver Research Institute, Center for Social Research and Development. 1975. *Socioeconomic Data and Change Measures for 1970 and 1972.* Denver, Colo.: University of Denver (March).

Donabedian, Avedis, and Leonard S. Rosenfeld. 1964. "Follow-up study of chronically ill patients discharged from hospital." *Journal of Chronic Diseases* 17:847–862.

Farina, A., H. Barry III, and M. Garnezy. 1963. "Birth order of recovered and nonrecovered schizophrenics." *Archives of General Psychiatry* 9:224.

Forssman, H., and I. Thuwe. 1966. "One hundred and twenty children born after application for therapeutic abortion refused." *Acta Psychiatrica Scandinavia* 42:71–78.

Frankenburg, W., J. Dodds, and A. Fandal. 1970. *Denver Developmental Screening Test Manual.* Denver: University of Colorado Medical Center (revised).

Frankenburg, W.; B.W. Camp; and P.A. Van Natta. 1971. "Validity of the Denver Developmental Screening Test." *Child Development* 42: 475–485.

Garbarino, James. 1976. "A preliminary study of some ecological correlates of child abuse: The impact of socioeconomic stress on mothers." *Child Development* 47:178–185.

Garbarino, James, and Ann Crouter. 1978. "Defining the community context for parent-child relations: The correlates of child maltreatment." *Child Development* 49:604–616.

Gil, D.G. 1970. *Violence Against Children: Physical Child Abuse in the U.S.* Cambridge, Mass.: Harvard University Press.

Giovannoni, Jeanne M., and Andrew Billingsley. 1970. "Child neglect among the poor: A study of parental adequacy in families of three ethnic groups." *Child Welfare* 44 no. 4:196–204.

Glaser, Barney G., and Anselm L. Strauss. 1967. *The Discovery of Grounded Theory: Strategies for Qualitative Research.* Chicago: Aldine.

Goldfarb. W. 1947. "Variations in adolescent adjustment in institutionally reared children." *American Journal of Orthopsychiatry* 17:449–457.

———. 1945. "Effects of psychological deprivation in infancy and subsequent stimulation." *American Journal of Psychiatry* 102:18–33.

Grant, M.W. 1964. "Family size." *British Journal of Social Medicine* 18:35–42.

Green, Lawrence W. 1970. "Status identity and preventive health behavior." *Pacific Health Education Reports.* Berkeley: School of Public Health, University of California.

Haggerty, Robert J.; Klaus J. Roghmann; and Ivan B. Pless. 1975. *Child Health and the Community.* New York: Wiley.

Haggerty, Robert J., and J.J. Alpert. 1963. "The child, his family and illness." *Post Graduate Medicine* 34:228–233.

Harlow, H.F. 1965. "Total social isolation: Effects on macaque monkey behavior." *Science* 148:666.

Harlow, H.F.; M.K. Harlow; and E.W. Hansen. 1963. "The maternal affectional system of rhesus monkeys," in H. Rheingold, ed. *Maternal Behavior in Mammals.* New York: Wiley.

Hegsted, D.M. 1972. "Problems in the use and interpretation of the recommended dietary allowances." *Ecology of Food and Nutrition* 1:255–265.

Heinzelmann, Fred, and Richard W. Bagley. 1970. "Response to physical activity programs and their effects on health behavior." *Public Health Reports 85,* no. 10 (October): 905–911.

Hepner, R., and N. Maiden. 1971. "Growth rate, nutrient intake & 'mothering' as determinants of malnutrition in disadvantaged children." *Nutrition Reviews* 29 (October):219–223.

Hurt, Maure, Jr. 1975. *Child Abuse and Neglect: A Report on the Status of the Research.* Washington, D.C.: Office of Human Development, Office of Child Development.

Jensen, G.D., and Tolman, C.W. 1962. "Mother-infant relationship in the monkey macaca memestrina: The effect of brief separation and mother-infant specificity." *Journal of Comparative Physiology and Psychology* 55:131–136.

Kempe, C. Henry. 1976. "Approaches to child abuse: The health visitor concept." *American Journal of Diseases of Children* 130 (September): 941–947.

Kempe, C.H., and R.E. Helfer, eds. 1972. *Helping the Battered Child and its Family.* Philadelphia: Lippincott.

Kessner, D.M.; J. Singer; C.E. Kalk; and E.R. Schlesinger. 1973. "Infant death: An analysis of maternal risk and health care," in *Contrasts in Health Status* 1. Washington, D.C.: Institute of Medicine, National Academy of Sciences.

Lieberman, E.J. 1970. "Reserving a womb: Case for the small family." *American Journal of Public Health* 60:87–92.

———. 1964. "Preventive psychiatry and family planning." *Journal of Marriage and the Family* 26:471.

MacMahon, Brian. 1974. "Infant mortality in the United States, " in C.L.

Erhardt and J.E. Berlin, eds., *Mortality and Morbidity in the United States*. Cambridge: Harvard University Press.

McClannahan, L.E. 1967. The Negro Unwed Mother: A Study of Adaptive Behavior. Unpublished Master's thesis, Department of Sociology, University of Wisconsin-Madison.

McKinlay, J.B. 1972. "Some approaches and problems in the study of the use of services: An overview." *Journal of Health and Social Behavior* 13 (June):115–152.

Madden, J.P.; S.J. Goodman; and H.A. Guthrie. 1976. "Validity of the 24-hour recall." *Journal of the American Dietetic Association* 68: 143–147.

Mechanic, D., and E.H. Volkart. 1961. "Stress, illness behavior, and the sick role." *American Sociological Review* 26 (February):51–58.

Mellinger, G.; D.I. Manheimer; and M.T. Kleman. 1967. *Deterrents to Adequate Immunization of Preschool Children*. Berkeley: Survey Research Center, University of California.

Menninger, K. 1943. "Psychiatric aspects of contraception." *Bulletin of the Menninger Clinic* 7:36.

Menken, Jane. 1972. "Health and social consequences of teen age child-bearing." *Family Planning Perspectives* 4 no. 3:45–53.

Morris, N.M.; M.H. Hatch; and S.S. Chipman. 1966. "Alienation as a deterrent to well-child supervision." *American Journal of Public Health* 56 (November):1874–1882.

National Center for Health Statistics (NCHS). 1980. Factors associated with low birth weight: United States 1976. *Vital and Health Statistics*. Series 21, No. 37. Washington, D.C.: Government Printing Office. (April)

———. 1978. *Health, United States 1978*. DHEW Publication No. (PHS) 78–1232. Washington, D.C.: Government Printing Office (December).

———. 1977a. *Health, United States 1976–1977*. DHEW Publication No. (HRA) 77–1232. Washington, D.C.: Government Printing Office.

———. 1977b. NCHS growth curves for children, birth–18 years, United States. *Vital and Health Statistics*. Series 11, No. 165. Washington, D.C.: Government Printing Office (November).

———. 1977c. Use of selected medical procedures associated with preventive care, United States 1973. *Vital and Health Statistics*. Series 10, No. 110. Washington, D.C.: Government Printing Office (March).

———. 1975. *Health, United States 1975*. Rockville, Md.: Public Health Service, Health Resources Administration.

———. 1969. International comparisons of medical care utilization: A feasibility study. By K.L. White and J. Murnaghan. *Vital and Health Statistics*. Series 2, No. 33. Washington, D.C.: Government Printing Office (June).

————. 1965. Physician visits: Interval of visits and children's routine checkup. United States July 1963–1965. *Vital and Health Statistics.* Series 10, No. 19. Washington, D.C.: Government Printing Office (June).

National Research Council. 1976. *Toward a National Policy for Children and Families.* Advisory Committee on Child Development. Washington, D.C.: National Academy of Sciences.

————. 1974. *Recommended Dietary Allowances,* 8th ed. Washington, D.C.: Food and Nutrition Council, National Academy of Sciences.

————. 1970. *Maternal Nutrition and the Course of Pregnancy.* Washington, D.C.: National Academy of Sciences.

Nutrition Reviews. 1977. "Infant feeding, somatic growth and obesity." 35 no. 9 (September):235–236.

————. 1976. "The validity of 24-hour dietary recalls." 34:310–311.

Oghalai, Karen. 1978. *Child Abuse in Wisconsin, 1977.* Madison, Wis.: Wisconsin Department of Health and Social Services, Division of Community Services.

Paige, D.M.; L. Davis; and A. Cordano. 1975. "Growth in disadvantaged black children." *Journal of School Health* 45 no. 3:161–164.

Palay, Miriam G. 1977. Census update, City of Milwaukee, 1975. Milwaukee: Milwaukee Urban Observatory, University of Wisconsin-Milwaukee.

Peters, E.N., and R.A. Hoekelman. 1973. "A measure of maternal competence." *HSMHA Health Reports* 88 (June–July):523–526.

Pilisuk, Marc, and Charles Froland. 1978. "Kinship, social networks, social support and health." *Social Science and Medicine* 12B no. 4: 273–280.

Pipes, Peggy. 1977. "When should semi-solid foods be fed to infants?" *Journal of Nutrition Education* 9 no. 2 (April–June): 57–59.

Pohlman, E.W. 1969. *The Psychology of Birth Planning,* Cambridge, Mass.: Schenkman.

————. 1965. "Results of unwanted conceptions: Some hypotheses up for adoption." *Eugenics Quarterly* 12:11–18.

Polansky, Norman A.; R.D. Borgman; and C. De Saix. 1972. *Roots of Futility.* San Francisco: Jossey-Bass.

Polansky, N.A.; C. De Saix; and S.A. Sharlin. 1972. *Child Neglect: Understanding and Reaching the Parent.* New York: Child Welfare League of America.

Polansky, N.A.; C. Hally; and N.F. Polansky. 1975. *Profile of Neglect: A Survey of the State of Knowledge of Child Neglect.* Washington, D.C.: Department of Health, Education and Welfare, Community Services Administration.

Provence, S., and R.C. Lipton. 1962. *Infants in Institutions.* New York: International Universities Press.

Read, Mary L. 1916. *The Mothercraft Manual.* Boston: Little, Brown.

Schooler, C. 1964. "Birth order and hospitalization for schizophrenia." *Journal of Abnormal Social Psychology* 69:574.

Seay, B., E. Hansen, and H.F. Harlow. 1962. "Mother-infant separation in monkeys." *Journal of Child Psychology and Psychiatry* 3:123-132.

Seay, B., and H.F. Harlow. 1965. "Maternal separation in the rhesus monkey." *Journal of Nervous and Mental Disorders* 140:434-441.

Shapiro, Sam; E.R. Schlesinger; and R.E.L. Nesbitt, Jr. 1968. *Infant, Perinatal, Maternal and Childhood Mortality in the United States.* Cambridge: Harvard University Press.

Silver, L.B.; C.C. Dublin; and R. Lourie. 1969. "Does violence beget violence: Contributions from a study of the child abuse syndrome." *American Journal of Psychiatry* 126 no. 3:404-407.

Slesinger, Doris P. 1980a. "Racial and residential differences in preventive medical care for infants in low-income populations." *Rural Sociology* 45 no. 1:69-90.

————. 1980b. "Rapid changes in household composition among low income mothers." *Family Relations* 29(April):221-228.

————. 1976. "The utilization of preventive medical services by urban black mothers," in D. Mechanic, ed., *The Growth of Bureaucratic Medicine.* New York: Wiley Interscience.

————. 1973a. "A Study of Infant Mortality in Wisconsin, 1969." Center for Demography and Ecology, University of Wisconsin-Madison. *Working Paper* 73-2 (May).

————. 1973b. The utilization of preventive medical services by urban black mothers: A sociocultural approach. Ph.D. dissertation, Department of Sociology, University of Wisconsin-Madison.

Slesinger, Doris P.; M. McDivitt; and F. O'Donnell. 1980. "Food patterns in an urban population: Age and sociodemographic correlates." *The Journal of Gerontology* 35 no. 3:432-441.

Slesinger, Doris P.; M. McDivitt; and J. Moorman. 1977. "Sociodemographic facts and food patterns affecting the nutritive quality of diets in an urban community." Center for Demography and Ecology, University of Wisconsin-Madison, *Working Paper* 77-14 (Spring).

Slesinger, D.P., and H.P. Travis. 1975. "A Study of Infant Mortality in Wisconsin, 1969 from Linked Birth and Death Records: An Application of Log-Linear Models." Center for Demography and Ecology, University of Wisconsin-Madison. *Working Paper* 75-15 (April).

Spence, J., W.S. Walton, F.J.W. Miller, and S.D.M. Court. 1954. *A*

Thousand Families in Newcastle upon Tyne. London: Oxford University Press.

Spitz, R.A. 1945. "Hospitalism: An inquiry into the genesis of psychiatric conditions in early childhood." *Psychoanalytic Study of the Child* 1:53–74.

Stuart, H.C. 1934. "Standards of physical development for reference in clinical appraisement." *Pediatrics* 5:194.

Thomas, A.; S. Chess; and H.G. Birch. 1968. *Temperament and Behavior Disorders in Children.* New York: New York University Press.

Thomas, A.; S. Chess; H.G. Birch; M.E. Hertzig; and S. Korn. 1963. *Behavioral Individuality in Early Childhood.* New York: New York University Press.

Trulson, M.F. 1955. "Assessment of dietary study methods II: Variability of eating practices and determination of sample size and duration of dietary surveys." *Journal of the American Dietetic Association* 31: 797–802.

Tulkin, S.R., and B.J. Cohler. 1973. "Childrearing attitudes and mother-child interaction in the first year of life." *Merrill-Palmer Quarterly* 19:95–106.

Tulkin, S.R., and J. Kagan. 1972. "Mother-child interaction in the first year of life." *Child Development* 43(March):31–41.

U.S. Bureau of the Census. 1971. *General Population Characteristics, Wisconsin.* 1970 Census of Population, PC(1)–B51. Washington, D.C.: Government Printing Office.

U.S. Department of Agriculture. 1970. *Food for Fitness. A Daily Food Guide.* Washington, D.C.: Government Printing Office, Leaflet No. 424 (revised).

U.S. Department of Health, Education and Welfare, Center for Disease Control. 1977a. "Recommendation of the public health service advisory committee on immunization practices: Diptheria and tetanus toxoids and pertussis vaccine." *Morbidity and Mortality Weekly Report* 26 no. 49 (December 9).

———. 1977b. "Recommendations of the public health service advisory committee on immunization practices: Poliomyelitis prevention." *Morbidity and Mortality Weekly Report* 26 no. 40 (October 7).

———. 1972. "Collected recommendations to the public health service advisory committee on immunization practices." *Morbidity and Mortality Weekly Report* 21 no. 25 (June 24).

U.S. Department of Health, Education and Welfare, Community Services Administration. 1975. *Poverty Guidelines in All States except Alaska and Hawaii.* Washington, D.C.: Government Printing Office.

U.S. Department of Health, Education and Welfare, National Center on

Child Abuse and Neglect. 1978. *1977 Analysis of Child Abuse and Neglect Research.* Washington, D.C.: Government Printing Office (January).

Werner, E.; K. Simonia; J.M. Bierman; and F.E. French. 1967. "Cumulative effect of perinatal complications and deprived environment on physical, intellectual and social development of pre-school children." *Pediatrics* 39 no. 4:490–505.

Wingerd, John, and Solomon Schoen. 1971. "Growth standards in the first 2 years of life based on measurements of white and black children in a prepaid health care program." *Pediatrics* 47 no. 5(May):818–825.

Wisconsin Department of Health and Social Services, Division of Health. 1975. *Wisconsin Physicians: Description, Distribution, 1973.* Madison (January).

Wisconsin Department of Health and Social Services, Division of Health, Nutrition Section. 1976. "Evaluation of nutritional adequacy of children's diets." Madison (April).

Yankauer, A.; W.E. Boek, E.D. Lawson; and F.A.J. Ianni. 1958. "Social stratification and health practices in childbearing and childrearing." *American Journal of Public Health* 48:732–741.

Yarrow, M.R. 1963. "Problems of methods in parent-child research." *Child Development* 34:215–226.

Index

Abortion, 6; denial of, 6
Accidents, baby, 46–47, 48, 58, 136; in
  control group, 181; and sociodemographic
  characteristics, 47; in vignettes, 65–66,
  74, 88–89, 92, 100; at waves one, two,
  and three, 46–47
Aday, Lu Ann, 139
Age of infant, 13–14, 15, 16, 145; in
  control group, 180; and growth
  standards, 43–44; and length, 43–44; and
  rural/urban residence, 15; at waves one,
  two, and three, 15, 16; and weight,
  43–44
Age of mother, 5, 24; and infant health
  measures, 58–59, 138; in matched sample,
  179; and mothercraft measures, 39, 40,
  104–106; by rural/urban residence, 22–23;
  and social integration, 122, 123, 124–126.
  See also Sociodemographic characteristics
Aid to Dependent Children (ADC), 24
Alpert, J.J., 6
American Academy of Pediatrics, 41
Andersen, Ronald, 139
Andrews, Frank, 103
Appalachia, 9, 136
Assessment of infant: health, 47–48, 58;
  physical and developmental, 9
Attitudes: and health knowledge, 105–106;
  and infant health measures, 59, 60;
  toward medical system, 28, 34–37; toward
  preventive care, 28, 35–36; of propensity
  to seek care, 28, 36–37; relationships
  among mothercraft components, 37, 38,
  39, scoring, 35–37; of skepticism toward
  doctors, 28, 35; and sociodemographic
  characteristics, 39, 40, 103, 105, 106. *See
  also* Mothercraft, measurement of

Beck, M.B., 5
Becker, Marshall H., 117
Bice, Thomas W., 36
Billingsley, Andrew, 3, 118
Birch, H.G., 3, 7
Birth certificate, 10, 11
Birthdates, infants, 11, 13
Birth order, 5, 138
Birthweight, 23, 43, 44; causal factors in, 1;
  in control group, 180, 183–184;
  prematurity and, 43; and prenatal diet, 1;
  by race, 1; by rural/urban residence,
  22–23, 139
Borgman, R.D., 4, 9
Boston-Stuart Series, 43
Breastfeeding, 50

Brown, G.W., 10
Bullough, Bonnie, 6, 118, 139

Center for Disease Control, 42
Charney, E., 51
Checkup. *See* Physical examination, infant
Chess, S., 3, 7
Child abuse, 6, 7, 142; National Center on,
  and Neglect, 142; and social isolation, 6;
  and wantedness of birth, 8
Childbearing history, 7; in vignettes, 63–101
Child development, 7, 9
Child health, 7, 9
Child neglect, 3, 4, 142–143; and nurturing,
  3; and removal from home, 15; and
  social support, 118; and wantedness of
  birth, 5
Children, number of: by rural/urban
  residence, 22–23, 24
Child Welfare League of America, Inc., 40
Chipman, S.S., 5, 6, 118
Church attendance, 118, 140; item, 119; and
  mothercraft measures, 120, 121, 126–133;
  and sociodemographic characteristics,
  122, 123. *See also* Social integration
Club membership: item, 119; and
  mothercraft measures, 120, 121, 124–126;
  and sociodemographic characteristics,
  122, 123
Cognitive care, 6, 28, 135. *See also*
  Mothercraft
Colds. *See* Illnesses, baby
Communicable diseases, 48, 181. *See also*
  Illnesses, baby
Community health workers, 7
Community resources: and sociocultural
  factors, 6. *See also* Social-service
  agencies
Confidentiality, 13
Control group, 145–146, 179–187
Cough. *See also* Illnesses, baby

Demographic characteristics. *See*
  Sociodemographic characteristics
Denver Developmental Screening Test
  (DDST), 9, 48–49, 58, 136, 145, 179; in
  control group, 182–183; delays in, 48–49;
  scoring, 48; at waves one, two, and three,
  48–49
Dependency. *See* Personality, maternal
De Saix, D., 4, 9, 40
Development, child, 48–49
Development, infant, 41–61, 145; measured
  in growth charts, 43–45; problems in, 48

197

Diet adequacy, 136, 141; and education, 139; measurement of, 52–53, 55, 56; and Mothercraft Component Score, 111, 114; and rural/urban residence, 139; and sociodemographic characteristics, 58, 59, 106–111, 112–113; in vignettes, 63–101

Diet of infant, 49–57, 58, 145; and eating schedule, 52, 57; and obesity, 51; at three months, 49–52; at twenty months, 52–57. *See also* Food groups, four basic

Diptheria, Pertussus, Tetanus (DPT), 42. *See also* Immunizations

Ear infection. *See* Illnesses, baby

Early and Periodic Screening, Diagnosis, and Treatment Program (EPSDT), 48

Eating schedule. *See* Diet of infant

Economic factors. *See* Sociodemographic characteristics

Education of mother, 5, 24, 141; and diet adequacy, 139; and infant health measures, 58–59, 138, 141; and mothercraft measures, 39, 40, 104–106; by rural/urban residence, 22–23; and social integration, 122–123, 124–126. *See also* Sociodemographic characteristics

Emotional handling, 6, 28, 135. *See also* Mothercraft; Mothercraft, measurement of

Exploratory study, 2, 3, 135

Extended family. *See* Household composition

Families, reasons for choosing, 11, 12

Family size, 5

Fels Research Institute, 43

Food groups, four basic: classification of, 52; comsumption of, at three months, 49–52; consumption of, at twenty months, 52–55; recommended intake of, 52–53, 55, 56; scoring of, 55; serving size of, 53. *See also* Diet of infant

Food stamps, 24

Foster mother, 15, 16, 142, 169, 172, 174

Frankenburg, W., 48

Friends and relatives. *See* Social integration; Visiting patterns

Garbarino, James, 6

Gill, D.G., 6

Giovannoni, Jeanne M., 3, 118

Green, L.W., 103, 117, 139

Grounded theory, 4

Growth charts, 179; in control group, 183–185. *See also* Length of infant; Weight of infant; Weight-for-length

Haggerty, Robert J., 3, 6, 7

Hatch, M.H., 5, 6, 118

Health, infant, 9, 41–61, 136, 138–139; family size and, 5; history of, 48; and mothercraft measures (MAS, MCS), 110–114, 126–133; nurse's rating of, 48; quality of mothering and, 4, 7; and sociodemographic characteristics, 58–59, 106–107, 108–109, 110–111, 112–113; summary measures of, 58; and wantedness of birth, 5. *See also* Assessment of infant; Nurse's assessment

Health information, 135; definition of, 33–34. *See also* Health knowledge; Mothercraft Component Score

Health knowledge, 4, 28, 135, 141; of baby care, 32–33; of disease, 33; index of, 33, 34; and infant health measures, 59, 60, 110–111, 112–113; and medical attitudes, 105–106; and relationship with mothercraft components, 37, 38; of safety, 34; and sociodemographic characteristics, 39, 40, 105–106, 110–111; in vignettes, 63–101, *See also* Mothercraft; Mothercraft, measurement of

Health status indicators, 45

Health visitor, 143–144

Height. *See* Length of infant

Hegsted, D.M., 52

Hepner, R., 4

Hoekelman, R.A., 34, 40, 110

Hospitalization of infant, 48; in surrogate cases, 170; in vignettes, 91–93, 97

Household composition, 6, 119, 139, 179; and mothercraft measures, 119, 121, 126–133; and preventive medical care, 118; by rural/urban residence, 22–23, 24; and sociodemographic characteristics, 122, 123

Husband, 24, 25, 139

Illnesses, baby, 46, 47, 58, 63–101, 136, 146; in control group, 181; and Mothercraft Component Score, 111, 114; and mothercraft measures, 59, 60, 126–133; number of, 46; and poverty, 139, 141; and rural/urban residence, 46, 47; scoring of, 46; and sociodemographic characteristics, 58, 59, 106–111; in vignettes, 78–79, 80–81, 96–97

Immunizations, 58, 136, 138–139, 146; in control group, 180; and Mothercraft Component Score, 111, 114; and mothercraft measures, 59, 60, 126–133; and poverty, 5, 6; and rural/urban residence, 42, 43; scoring of, 42, 43; and social isolation, 118; and sociodemographic characteristics, 58, 59, 106–111, 112–113; standards of DPT, Polio, Rubella, 42, 43; in vignettes, 63–101; at wave three, 42

Income, 5; of family, 24; and illness, 103;

and immunizations, 5; and infant medical care, 6; redundancy with poverty, 104; by rural/urban residence, 22–23. *See also* Poverty; Sociodemographic characteristics
Infant: birthweight of, 23; and preventive health measures, 41–42; sex of, 20
Infant morbidity, 2; postneonatal, 2
Infant mortality, 1–2; and age of mother, 5
Integration, primary and secondary, 137; definition of, 117; measures of, 119; and mothercraft measures, 119–121, 124–126; and sociodemographic characteristics, 122. *See also* Social integration
Interaction, mother-infant, 7
Interviews: at home visits, 9, 138; and mothercraft appraisal score, 29–32; and thumbnail sketch, 13; at waves one, two, and three, 13
Interview schedule, 147–162
Interviewer training, 11–13

Kagan, J., 3, 4
Kempe, C.H., 3, 144

Lead poisoning, 66, 71–72, 143, 181
Length of infant, 9; by age, 43–45; at birth, 43–44; in control group, 183–185; as health-status indicator, 45; at waves one, two, and three, 43, 44, 45
London, England, 10
Longitudinal study, 7, 13, 142

McDivitt, M., 52
McKinlay, J.B., 5
Male partner, 24
Marital status of mother, 24; in matched sample, 179; by rural/urban residence, 22–23
Mashfield Clinic, 18
Maternal deprivation, 3
Measurement of mothering, 9
Mechanic, D., 36
Medicaid, 24
Medical facilities: in Milwaukee, 17; in four rural counties, 18, 21
Mellinger, G., 6
Methodology, 9–16, 137–138; combination of interview and observation in, 9–10; reliability, 29. *See also* Sample
Metropolitan residence, 10, 22–23. *See also* Urban residence
Milk intake: obesity and, 51; at three months, 49–50, 51, 52; at twenty months, 53, 54, 55, 56; type of, 50. *See also* Breastfeeding; Diet of infant
Milwaukee, Wis., 10–11, 42, 64, 70, 73, 76 80, 83, 99; Bureau of Public Health Nursing, 10, 179, 186; Department of Public Welfare, 186; Health Department, 10; medical facilities in, 17;

neighborhoods, 17, 18, 19; sample, 11, 17, 18
Model of mothering, 4, 5, 136–137
Moorman, J., 52
Morris, N.M., 5, 6, 118
Mortality, *See* Infant mortality
Mother: biological, 3; social, economic and demographic characteristics of, 23–25; surrogate for, 3
Mothercraft, 4, 7, 27–40; components of, 4, 27–28, 135; concept of, 4, 7; definition of, 4; and infant health, 110–111, 112–113, 126–133; measures of, 37–40; relationships among components of, 37, 38, 39; and social integration, 119–121, 124–126, 140; and sociodemographic characteristics, 39, 40, 59, 60, 110–111, 112–113. *See also* Mothering; Mothercraft appraisal score
Mothercraft appraisal, 138–141; and social integration, 119–121, 124–126; in vignettes, 63–101
Mothercraft appraisal form, 136, 138, 163–168; scoring of, 163–168
Mothercraft Appraisal Score (MAS), 4, 27–28, 137, 138; apathy-futility in, 31–32; cleanliness and dress in, 30; correlations between waves of, 32, 33, 137; dependency in, 31; evaluation of items in, 175–177; feeding in, 30; handling of child in, 31; housing adequacy in, 29; and infant health measures, 59, 60, 110–111, 112–113, 126–133; items, 29–32; material attributes in, 30; medical care in, 30; relationships among components of, 37, 38; reliability test of, 175–177; rest in, 30; safety and cleanliness in home and, 29; scoring of, 32, 137; stimulation of child in, 31; and social integration, 119–121, 124–133; and sociodemographic characteristics, 104–105, 110–111, 112–113; verbal communication in, 32. *See also* Mothercraft Component Score
Mothercraft Component Score (MCS), 111 114–115; comparison with mothercraft appraisal score (MAS), 111; and infant health measures, 111, 114, 126–133; and social integration, 119–121, 124–133; and sociodemographic characteristics, 111, 115
Mothercraft, measurement of: attitudes, 34–37; emotional and cognitive care (MAS), 31; health knowledge, 32–34; and infant health measures, 110–111, 112–113; medical care (MAS), 30; Mothercraft Component Score, 111, 114–115; by Mothercraft Appraisal Score (MAS) at waves one, two, and three, 29; personality of mother (MAS),

31–32; physical environment (MAS), 29–30; physical needs (MAS), 30; propensity to seek care, 36–37; and social integration, 119–121, 124–126; sociodemographic characteristics, 59, 60, 110–111, 112–113
Mothering, 7; concept of, 4; and infant health, 4, 7; measurement of, 9; model of, 4, 136; quality of, 3–5, 135–137; and sociodemographic characteristics, 5. See also Mothercraft
Multiple Classification Analysis (MCA), 103

National Center for Health Statistics (NCHS), 1, 2, 6, 23, 36, 43, 103, 139
National Research Council, 1, 2–3, 53, 141
Neonatal deaths, 2
Nonmetropolitan residence, 10, 22–23; definition of, 18. See also Rural residence
Nurse. See Public-health nurse
Nurse's assessment, 136, 138, 179; in control group, 182, 183; and Mothercraft Component Score, 111, 114; and mothercraft measures, 59, 60, 126–133; and sociodemographic characteristics, 58, 59, 106–111, 112–113; in vignettes, 63–101; at wave three, 47–48, 58
Nurturing, 3; ability, 4
Nutrition. See Diet of infant
Nutritional standards, 52–53

Obesity, 45, 51, 139; and diet, 51, 56, 145; and race, 141; at wave one, 51; at wave three, 56
O'Donnell, F., 52

Personality, maternal: apathy-futility, 4, 135; dependency, 4, 31, 135; disorders, 3, 135, verbal communication, 4, 135. See also Mothercraft; Mothercraft Appraisal Score; Mothercraft, measurement of
Peters, E.N., 34, 110
Physical care of child, 7, 28, 135. See also Mothercraft; Mothercraft, measurement of
Physical environment, 6, 27, 135. See also Mothercraft; Mothercraft, measurement of
Physical examination, infant, 9, 41, 58, 136, 138–139; history of, 41, 42; and Mothercraft Component Score, 111, 114; and mothercraft measures, 59, 60, 126–133; by nurse, 47–48; and poverty, 6; by rural/urban residence, 41, 42; scoring, 41, 42; and sociodemographic characteristics, 58, 59, 106–111, 112–113;

in vignettes, 63–101
Pless, Ivan B., 3, 7
Polansky, N.A., 4, 9, 29, 31, 32, 40, 136
Polio, 42. See also Immunizations
Population characteristics: in four rural counties, 17–18, 21; of Milwaukee neighborhoods, 17, 19
Postneonatal death, 2; and race, 2
Poverty, 7; and infant deaths, 2; and immunizations, 6; in selection of sample, 10; and well-baby checkups, 6
Poverty of mother, 24, 138, 141; and illnesses, baby, 139, 141; and infant health measures, 58–59; and mothercraft measures, 39, 40, 104–106; by rural/urban residence, 22–23; and social integration, 122–123, 124–126. See also Sociodemographic characteristics
Prematurity: and birthweight, 43; and length, 45
Prenatal care, 5; and birthweight, 1; in high-risk clinic, 11
Preventive health care, 6, 145; for infant, 41–42; and mothercraft, 141; and social integration, 6
Preventive medical utilization: and sociodemographic characteristics, 103
Prospective study, 7, 135
Public assistance: and abortion, 6; received by mother, 24; by rural/urban residence, 22–23
Public-health nurse, 7, 10–12, 43, 50, 137, 138, 140, 143, 175, 186; as interviewer, 9, 11–13, 29, 32, 34, 41; neonatal assessment by, 10

Qualitative ratings, 7

Race: and birthweight, 1; infant death rates by, 2; and infant health measures, 58–59; of infants in control group, 180; length by, 43; in matched sample, 179; of mother, 24; and mothercraft measures, 39, 40, 104–106; and postneonatal deaths, 2; and preventive medical care, 118; and social integration, 122, 123, 124–126; by rural/urban residence, 22–23; in urban sample, 6; weight by, 43. See also Sociodemographic characteristics
Rash. See Illnesses, baby
Read, Mary, L., 27
Residential mobility, 14, 15, 139; in vignettes, 65–66, 77–78, 84, 100
Roghmann, Klaus J., 3, 7
Rubella, 42, 186–187. See also Immunizations
Rural residence, 9, 15, 67, 87, 90, 95; age of infants at interviews by, 15, 16; counties of, 10, 11; demographic and economic characteristics of infants and

mothers having, 20, 22–25; and infant
health measures, 58–59, 138–139; and
mothercraft measures, 39, 40, 104–106;
population characteristics of, 21; of
sample mothers, 11, 17–18, 20; and social
integration, 122, 123, 124–126. *See also*
Sociodemographic characteristics

Safety information, 135; and infant health
measures, 110–111, 112–113;
measurement of, 29, 34, 35; and
sociodemographic characteristics,
105–106; in vignettes, 63–101. *See also*
Mothercraft Component Score
Sample, 7, 10–11, 137–138; deterioration,
14; geographical location of, 17; in
Milwaukee, 11, 17, 18; in rural counties,
11, 17–18, 20; size of, 11, 16; wave three,
16. *See also* Methodology
Sample selection, 138; and age of infant,
11; and maternal characteristics, 11;
by nurses, 11, 12; through screening
families, 10, 11
Sex of infant, 20; in control group, 180;
by rural/urban residence, 22–23
Sharlin, S.A., 4, 40
Silver, L.B., 5
Slesinger, Doris P., 1, 6, 36, 52, 103, 118,
119, 127, 139
Snack foods, 50, 55–56, 57
Social environment. *See* Sociocultural
characteristics
Social integration, 6, 139–140; and infant
health measures, 126–133; measures of,
118–119; and mothercraft measures,
119–121, 141–142; and preventive health
care, 6; and propensity to seek medical
care, 6; and sociodemographic
characteristics, 122–133; and utilization
of medical services, 117–118; in
vignettes, 63–101
Social isolation, 3, 118; and child abuse, 6;
and medical utilization, 6, 118; and
stress, 6; in vignettes, 66, 87. *See also*
Social integration
Social-service agencies, 185–186;
involvement with, 143–144, 146; workers
from, 11
Social support, 4, 6, 118, 137. *See also*
Social integration
Socializing: item, 119; and mothercraft
measures, 120, 121; and
sociodemographic characteristics, 122,
123
Sociocultural characteristics, 4–7, 117–133,
137, 139; quality of mothering and, 4, 5;
and social institutions, 6. *See also*
Social integration
Sociodemographic characteristics, 4, 5, 7,
103–115, 137, 138; and accidents, 47;

and components of mothercraft, 39–40,
103–106, 110–111; and health knowledge,
105–106; of infant, 20, 22–23; and infant
health, 58–59, 110–111, 126–133; and
medical attitudes, 105–106; of mother,
22–23, 23–25; and Mothercraft
Component Score, 111, 115; and
mothercraft measures, 127–133; and
quality of mothering, 4, 5, 140; and
social integration, 122–123. *See also*
Age of mother; Education of mother;
Poverty of mother; Race; Rural
residence; Urban residence
Socioeconomic characteristics. *See*
Sociodemographic characteristics
Sociological perspective, 7
Spence, J., 6, 9
Stress, 6; and social isolation, 6; and
streptococcal infections, 6–7; and
utilization of medical services, 7
Structural constraints, 4
Sudden Infant Death Syndrome, 16
Surgery, infant, 48, 181
Surrogate mother, 3, 16, 142; cases,
169–174
Sweden, 5–6

Teen-age pregnancy: program, 11; in
surrogate cases, 170, 172; in vignettes,
80–82
Thomas, A., 3, 7
Thumbnail sketch, 13
Time schedule of project, 13–14
Tulkin, S.R., 3, 4
Twenty-four hour food recall, 52

U.S. Bureau of the Census, 18
U.S. Department of Agriculture (USDA),
52, 53, 55
Urban residence, 6, 9, 15; age of infant at
interviews by, 15, 16; demographic and
economic characteristics of infants and
mothers having, 20, 22–25; and infant
health measures, 58–59, 138–139; and
mothercraft measures, 39, 40, 104–106;
population characteristics of Milwaukee
neighborhoods, 17, 19; of sample
mothers, 17, 18; and social integration,
122, 123, 124–126. *See also* Milwaukee,
Wis.; Sociodemographic characteristics
Utilization of medical services, 9; and
education, 138–139; and family size, 5;
postnatal, 5; prenatal, 5; and social
integration, 117–118
Utilization of medical services for infant, 9;
and family income, 6; and social
isolation, 6; and stress, 7

Verbal communication, 4. *See also*
Personality, maternal

Visiting patterns, 118; item, 119; and
  mothercraft measures, 120, 121, 124–126;
  and sociodemographic characteristics,
  122, 123. *See also* Social integration
Vitamins, 50, 51

Wantedness of birth, 5–6; in vignettes, 64,
  67–69, 70–72, 73, 78, 80, 87, 90
Weight-for-length, 51, 56, 58, 136, 139,
  141; in control group, 183–185; and diet,
  51–52; as health-status indicator, 45; and
  Mothercraft Component Score, 111, 114;
  and mothercraft measures, 59, 60,
  126–133; obesity and, 45; and
  sociodemographic characteristics, 58, 59,
  106–111; in vignettes, 79, 85, 89, 94; at

waves one, two, and three, 43–46, 45
Weight of infant, 9; by age, 43–45; at birth,
  43–44; in control group, 183–185; as
  health-status indicator, 45; at waves one,
  two, and three, 43, 44, 45
Wisconsin, 17; child abuse in, 142; location
  of study families in, 20; nutrition guide
  by, 52
Wisconsin Department of Public Health
  Nursing, 10
Wisconsin Division of Protective Services,
  15, 16, 170
Work experience, 119, 140; and mothercraft
  measures, 120, 121, 126–133; and
  sociodemographic characteristics, 122,
  123

About the Author

Doris P. Slesinger is associate professor in the Department of Rural Sociology, University of Wisconsin, Madison. Her fields of specialization include demography, medical sociology, and applied sociology.

She graduated from Vassar College in 1949, received the M.A. from the University of Michigan in 1960, and the Ph.D. in sociology from the University of Wisconsin, Madison, in 1973. This was followed by a Robert Wood Johnson postdoctoral fellowship at the Center for Medical Sociology, University of Wisconsin, Madison.

Her research has centered on the health status and medical-utilization patterns of underserved populations. She has studied urban black mothers and their use of preventive medical care for their children and themselves. She has completed a survey of unmet health needs of Mexican-American migrant agricultural workers in Wisconsin. She plans to investigate maternal and infant health-care patterns in a small city and surrounding rural area in the coastal region of Peru during 1981–1982.

She has special concern with women's understanding of their bodies and health, and she has published a number of health-education brochures on vaginal infections, venereal disease, sterilization and menopause, all written from the patient's perspective. Available in English and Spanish, they are widely distributed throughout the United States at family-planning centers, women's health clinics, and neighborhood clinics.

She is currently codirector of the Applied Population Laboratory of the Department of Rural Sociology, and also codirector of the Wisconsin State Data Center, a federal-state cooperative program with the U.S. Bureau of the Census.